THE SHADOW-LANDS OF C. S. LEWIS

The Shadow-Lands of C. S. Lewis

The Man behind the Movie

Edited by
Peter Kreeft

IGNATIUS PRESS   SAN FRANCISCO

Cover photograph of C. S. Lewis
is from the Marion E. Wade Center,
Wheaton College, Wheaton, Illinois

Cover design by Riz Boncan Marsella

© 1994, Ignatius Press, San Francisco
All rights reserved
ISBN 0–89870–493–6
Library of Congress catalogue number 94–75772
Printed in the United States of America

Contents

Introduction 11

I. SHADOW-LANDS

This World as "Shadow-Lands" 15
"Meditation in a Toolshed": "Looking Along" vs.
   "Looking At" (from *God in the Dock*) 17
"Back on This Side of the Door" (from *The Lion,*
   the Witch and the Wardrobe) 20
"The Queen of Underland" (from *The Silver Chair*) . . . 24
Meeting an Angel (from *Perelandra*) 32
"Allegory" (from *The Allegory of Love*) 35
"The Magician's Book" (from *The Voyage of the*
   Dawn Treader) 37
"Patches of Godlight" (from *Letters to Malcolm*) 39
"Think of Yourself as a Seed" (from *Letters to an*
   American Lady) 41

II. JOY

The Mysterious Longing ("Joy") 45
Two Mysteries of Desire (from the Preface to
   The Pilgrim's Regress) 47
Reading the Riddle, Following the Clue
   (from *Surprised by Joy*, Lewis' autobiography) 51
"Hope" (from *Mere Christianity*) 66
"The Weight of Glory": Weaving the Spell of
   Good Magic (from "The Weight of Glory") 71
Happiness, Not Unhappiness, Begets Longing
   (from *Till We Have Faces*) 76
The Preciousness of Longing (from *Poems*) 77

III. HEAVEN

"The Land from Which the Shadows Fall"
(Heaven) 81
"Immortal Horrors or Everlasting Splendours"
(from "The Weight of Glory") 83
"Man or Rabbit?" (from *God in the Dock*) 87
Is Heaven Playful or Serious? (from *Letters to
Malcolm*) 88
A Modern Mini-*Divine Comedy* (from *The Great
Divorce*) 90
"Further Up and Further In" (from *The Last Battle*) ... 94
"Farewell to Shadow-Lands" (from *The Last Battle*) 99
"Heaven" (from *The Problem of Pain*) 104

IV. THE GOLDEN KEY

"The Golden Key" to "The Land from Which the
Shadows Fall" 117
"The Golden Key" by George MacDonald 119
Lord, Liar, or Lunatic? (from *Mere Christianity*) 160
"What Are We to Make of Jesus Christ?" (from *God
in the Dock*) 164
The Lamb and the Lion (from *The Voyage of the
Dawn Treader*) 171
"They Went All Trembly" (from *The Lion, the Witch
and the Wardrobe*) 173

V. THE PROBLEM OF PAIN

"The Problem of Pain" 177
Explaining Pain (from *The Problem of Pain*) 179
Experiencing Pain (from *A Grief Observed*) 190
"Footnote to All Prayers" (from *Poems*) 202

CONTENTS

"The Apologist's Evening Prayer" (from *Poems*) 203

"No Earthly Comfort" (from *Poems*) 204

"No Safe Investment" (from *The Four Loves*) 206

"We Shall Find Them All in Him" (from *The Four Loves*) 207

Conclusion: Realism or Idealism? 211

Suggestions for Further Reading 213

Acknowledgments 219

To the sublime Plato
who showed us a world outside the Cave
but could not take us there

Introduction

IN THIS BOOK you will read some of the most beautiful and moving passages of English prose ever written about some of the most mysterious and precious experiences you have ever felt:

—the haunting sense that this whole world is a "Shadow-Land";

—the innate longing for "something more" that always escapes labels and definitions, whether theological or psychological;

—soaring imagination and clear reason working in tandem to suggest some hints of this "land from which the shadows fall";

—a knockout argument that we already have "the golden key" to this land in our grasp; and

—the jarring, jolting, Monday-morning, cancer-ridden, doubt-haunted world that seems to give the lie to this whole worldview as merely a desperate escapist fantasy (but does not).

This anthology is a necklace of gems from C. S. Lewis' mine of some fifty books. Its unifying principle is the point of the title of the movie *Shadowlands*, in five steps, as summarized above. I compiled it especially for those who wonder what Lewis himself wrote about these things, to give you an opportunity to meet the mind of the man behind the movie without reading all fifty books.

I

SHADOW-LANDS

"We live in the Shadowlands."

— *"Shadowlands"* (the movie)

This World as "Shadow-Lands"

THERE ARE TWO PHILOSOPHIES about this whole world. One says this is all there is. The other says there is more. C. S. Lewis calls these two philosophies Naturalism and Supernaturalism. His two most philosophical (and difficult) books, *Miracles* and *The Abolition of Man*, argue for Supernaturalism: for a God and a moral law transcendent to the material universe. But the excerpts here give you not the *arguments* but the *intuition*, the sense that what we see is like a shadow: it is real, but it points beyond itself, like a sign, to something more behind it, or above it, or within it—like the human face, or great music.

Supernaturalism has been the philosophy of 99% of all human beings who have ever lived before the twentieth century. It is still held by about 90% of the people alive today. But it is believed only by a small minority of people in the three main mind-molding institutions in Western civilization: education, entertainment, and journalism. One of the reasons for its decline is surely the loss, or suppression, of the *sense* of the world as shadow-lands, as shadow, as sign, as full of *sign*ificance. Lewis helps restore this sense.

"Meditation in a Toolshed":
"Looking Along" vs. "Looking At"

This first little essay is in a way the key to all the rest, for it identifies the kind of consciousness we need to cultivate if we are to "look *along*" the shadow rather than to "look *at*" it like a dog staring at your finger while you point to his dog house.

———

I WAS STANDING TODAY in the dark toolshed. The sun was shining outside and through the crack at the top of the door there came a sunbeam. From where I stood that beam of light, with the specks of dust floating in it, was the most striking thing in the place. Everything else was almost pitch-black. I was seeing the beam, not seeing things by it.

Then I moved, so that the beam fell on my eyes. Instantly the whole previous picture vanished. I saw no toolshed, and (above all) no beam. Instead I saw, framed in the irregular cranny at the top of the door, green leaves moving on the branches of the tree outside and beyond that, 90 odd million miles away, the sun. Looking along the beam, and looking at the beam are very different experiences.

But this is only a very simple example of the differ-

God in the Dock: Essays on Theology and Ethics, ed. Walter Hooper (Grand Rapids, Mich.: Wm. B. Eerdmans, 1970), pp. 212–13.

ence between looking at and looking along. A young man meets a girl. The whole world looks different when he sees her. Her voice reminds him of something he has been trying to remember all his life, and ten minutes casual chat with her is more precious than all the favours that all other women in the world could grant. He is, as they say, 'in love'. Now comes a scientist and describes this young man's experience from the outside. For him it is all an affair of the young man's genes and a recognised biological stimulus. That is the difference between looking *along* the sexual impulse and looking *at* it. . . .

❧

As soon as you have grasped this simple distinction, it raises a question. You get one experience of a thing when you look along it and another when you look at it. Which is the 'true' or 'valid' experience? Which tells you most about the thing? And you can hardly ask that question without noticing that for the last fifty years or so everyone has been taking the answer for granted. It has been assumed without discussion that if you want the true account of religion you must go, not to religious people, but to anthropologists; that if you want the true account of sexual love you must go, not to lovers, but to psychologists; that if you want to understand some 'ideology' (such as medieval chivalry or the nineteenth-century idea of a 'gentleman'), you must listen not to those who lived inside it, but to sociologists.

The people who look *at* things have had it all their own way; the people who look *along* things have simply been brow-beaten. It has even come to be taken for granted that the external account of a thing somehow refutes or 'debunks' the account given from inside. 'All these moral ideals which look so transcendental and beautiful from inside', says the wiseacre, 'are really only a mass of biological instincts and inherited taboos.' And no one plays the game the other way round by replying, 'If you will only step inside, the things that look to you like instincts and taboos will suddenly reveal their real and transcendental nature.'

"Back on This Side of the Door"

Lewis' most popular books are his children's stories, the seven Chronicles of Narnia. *The Lion, the Witch and the Wardrobe*, the first of the seven, was recently voted their first choice and favorite book by a nationwide poll of American children.

In this book, Lucy (and later her three siblings) go through a magic wardrobe into another world, Narnia. The existence of other worlds and of doors into them (Like Alice's rabbit-hole and looking-glass) holds an instinctive fascination for adults as well as children, for the two most important things that happen to all of us—birth and death—are like that.

In the following excerpt, a wise old professor (Lewis' mouthpiece) offers a startlingly simple argument for believing that there *are* other worlds like Narnia. Lewis uses the same argument later (see Part IV, pp. 163–70) for believing a claim as incredible as Lucy's, a claim made by a man who claims to have come from another world and even to *be* the wardrobe, or the Door, or the "golden key" to this other world.

S O THEY WENT AND KNOCKED at the study door, and the Professor said "Come in," and got up and found chairs for them and said he was quite at their disposal. Then he sat listening to them with the tips of his fingers pressed together and never interrupting, till they had fin-

The Lion, the Witch and the Wardrobe (New York: Macmillan, 1950), pp. 37–40.

ished the whole story. After that he said nothing for quite a long time. Then he cleared his throat and said the last thing either of them expected.

"How do you know?" he asked, "that your sister's story is not true?"

"Oh, but—" began Susan, and then stopped. Anyone could see from the old man's face that he was perfectly serious. Then Susan pulled herself together and said, "But Edmund said they had only been pretending."

"That is a point," said the Professor, "which certainly deserves consideration; very careful consideration. For instance—if you will excuse me for asking the question—does your experience lead you to regard your brother or your sister as the more reliable? I mean, which is the more truthful?"

"That's just the funny thing about it, Sir," said Peter. "Up till now, I'd have said Lucy every time."

"And what do you think, my dear?" said the Professor, turning to Susan.

"Well," said Susan, "in general, I'd say the same as Peter, but this couldn't be true—all this about the wood and the Faun."

"That is more than I know," said the Professor, "and a charge of lying against someone whom you have always found truthful is a very serious thing; a very serious thing indeed."

"We were afraid it mightn't even be lying," said Susan. "We thought there might be something wrong with Lucy."

"Madness, you mean?" said the Professor quite coolly. "Oh, you can make your minds easy about that. One has only to look at her and talk to her to see that she is not mad."

"But then," said Susan and stopped. She had never dreamed that a grown-up would talk like the Professor and didn't know what to think.

"Logic!" said the Professor half to himself. "Why don't they teach logic at these schools? There are only three possibilities. Either your sister is telling lies, or she is mad, or she is telling the truth. You know she doesn't tell lies and it is obvious that she is not mad. For the moment then and unless any further evidence turns up, we must assume that she is telling the truth."

Susan looked at him very hard and was quite sure from the expression of his face that he was not making fun of them.

"But how could it be true, Sir?" said Peter

"Why do you say that?" asked the Professor.

"Well, for one thing," said Peter, "if it was real why doesn't everyone find this country every time they go to the wardrobe? I mean, there was nothing there when we looked; even Lucy didn't pretend there was."

"What has that to do with it?" said the Professor.

"Well, Sir, if things are real, they're there all the time."

"Are they?" said the Professor; and Peter did not know quite what to say.

"But there was no time," said Susan, "Lucy had had no time to have gone anywhere, even if there was such a place. She came running after us the very moment we were out of the room. It was less than a minute, and she pretended to have been away for hours."

"That is the very thing that makes her story so likely

to be true," said the Professor. "If there really is a door in this house that leads to some other world (and I should warn you that this is a very strange house, and even I know very little about it)—if, I say, she had got into another world, I should not be at all surprised to find that that other world had a separate time of its own; so that however long you stayed there it would never take up any of *our* time. On the other hand, I don't think many girls of her age would invent that idea for themselves. If she had been pretending, she would have hidden for a reasonable time before coming out and telling her story."

"But do you really mean, Sir," said Peter, "that there could be other worlds—all over the place, just round the corner—like that?"

"Nothing is more probable," said the Professor, taking off his spectacles and beginning to polish them, while he muttered to himself, "I wonder what they *do* teach them at these schools."

"The Queen of Underland"

In the following passage from *The Silver Chair*, the wicked witch, like many modern educators, tries to lay a spell on the children imprisoned in her underground kingdom to make them forget the reality of the greater world of Narnia outside. What Narnia is to the witch's underworld, Heaven is to earth, the "Shadow-Lands".

In the end, only pain brings the children out of their illusion. (Compare the passage from *The Problem of Pain* on p. 186.)

N OW THE WITCH SAID NOTHING AT ALL, but moved gently across the room, always keeping her face and eyes very steadily towards the Prince. When she had come to a little ark set in the wall not far from the fireplace, she opened it, and took out first a handful of a green powder. This she threw on the fire. It did not blaze much, but a very sweet and drowsy smell came from it. And all through the conversation which followed, that smell grew stronger, and filled the room, and made it harder to think. Secondly, she took out a musical instrument rather like a mandolin. She began to play it with her fingers— a steady, monotonous thrumming that you didn't notice after a few minutes. But the less you noticed it, the more it got into your brain and your blood. This also made it hard to think. After she had thrummed for a time (and

The Silver Chair (New York: Macmillan, 1953), pp. 147–55.

the sweet smell was now strong) she began speaking in a sweet, quiet voice.

"Narnia?" she said. "Narnia? I have often heard your Lordship utter that name in your ravings. Dear Prince, you are very sick. There is no land called Narnia."

"Yes there is though, Ma'am," said Puddleglum. "You see, I happen to have lived there all my life."

"Indeed," said the Witch. "Tell me, I pray you, where that country is?"

"Up there," said Puddleglum, stoutly, pointing overhead. "I—I don't know exactly where."

"How?" said the Queen, with a kind, soft, musical laugh, "Is there a country up among the stones and mortar of the roof?"

"No," said Puddleglum, struggling a little to get his breath. "It's in Overworld."

"And what, or where, pray is this . . . how do you call it *Overworld*?"

"Oh don't be so silly," said Scrubb, who was fighting hard against the enchantment of the sweet smell and the thrumming, "As if you didn't know! It's up above, up where you can see the sky and the sun and the stars. Why, you've been there yourself. We met you there."

"I cry you mercy, little brother," laughed the Witch (you couldn't have heard a lovelier laugh). "I have no memory of that meeting. But we often meet our friends in strange places when we dream. And unless all dreamed alike, you must not ask them to remember it."

"Madam," said the Prince sternly, "I have already told your Grace that I am the King's son of Narnia."

"And shalt be, dear friend," said the Witch in a soothing voice, as if she was humouring a child, "shalt be king of many imagined lands in thy fancies."

"We've been there, too," snapped Jill. She was very angry because she could feel enchantment getting hold of her every moment. But of course the very fact that she could still feel it, showed that it had not yet fully worked.

"And thou art Queen of Narnia too, I doubt not, pretty one," said the Witch in the same coaxing, half-mocking tone.

"I'm nothing of the sort," said Jill, stamping her foot. "*We* come from another world."

"Why, this is a prettier game than the other," said the Witch. "Tell us, little maid, where is this other world? What ships and chariots go between it and ours?"

Of course a lot of things darted into Jill's head at once: Experiment House, Adela Pennyfather, her own home, radio-sets, cinemas, cars, aeroplanes, ration-books, queues. But they seemed dim and far away. (*Thrum—thrum—thrum*—went the strings of the Witch's instrument.) Jill couldn't remember the names of the things in our world. And this time it didn't come into her head that she was being enchanted, for now the magic was in its full strength; and of course, the more enchanted you get, the more certain you feel that you are not enchanted at all. She found herself saying (and at the moment it was a relief to say):

"No. I suppose that other world must be all a dream."

"Yes. It *is* all a dream," said the Witch, always thrumming.

"Yes, all a dream," said Jill.

"There never was such a world," said the Witch.

"No," said Jill and Scrubb, "never was such a world."

"There never was any world but mine," said the Witch.

"There never was any world but yours," said they.

Puddleglum was still fighting hard. "I don't know rightly what you all mean by a world," he said, talking like a man who hasn't enough air. "But you can play that fiddle till your fingers drop off, and still you won't make me forget Narnia; and the whole Overworld too. We'll never see it *again*, I shouldn't wonder. You may have blotted it out and turned it dark like this, for all I know. Nothing more likely. But I know I was there once. I've seen the sky full of stars. I've seen the sun coming up out of the sea of a morning and sinking behind the mountains at night. And I've seen him up in the midday sky when I couldn't look at him for brightness."

Puddleglum's words had a very rousing effect. The other three all breathed again and looked at one another like people newly awaked.

"Why, there it is!" cried the Prince. "Of course! The blessing of Aslan upon this honest Marsh-wiggle. We have all been dreaming, these last few minutes. How could we have forgotten it? Of course we've all seen the sun."

"By Jove, so we have!" said Scrubb. "Good for you, Puddleglum! You're the only one of us with any sense, I do believe."

Then came the Witch's voice, cooing softly like the voice of a wood-pigeon from the high elms in an old garden at three o'clock in the middle of a sleepy, summer afternoon; and it said:

"What is this *sun* that you all speak of? Do you mean anything by the word?"

"Yes, we jolly well do," said Scrubb.

"Can you tell me what it's like?" asked the Witch (*thrum, thrum, thrum,* went the strings).

"Please it your Grace," said the Prince, very coldly and politely. "You see that lamp. It is round and yellow and gives light to the whole room; and hangeth moreover from the roof. Now that thing which we call the sun is like the lamp, only far greater and brighter. It giveth light to the whole Overworld and hangeth in the sky."

"Hangeth from what, my lord?" asked the Witch; and then, while they were all still thinking how to answer her, she added, with another of her soft, silver laughs. "You see? When you try to think out clearly what this *sun* must be, you cannot tell me. You can only tell me it is like the lamp. Your *sun* is a dream; and there is nothing in that dream that was not copied from the lamp. The lamp is the real thing; the *sun* is but a tale, a children's story."

"Yes, I see now," said Jill in a heavy, hopeless tone. "It must be so." And while she said this, it seemed to her to be very good sense.

Slowly and gravely the Witch repeated, "There is no *sun.*" And they all said nothing. She repeated, in a softer and deeper voice. "There is no *sun.*" After a pause, and after a struggle in their minds, all four of them said together. "You are right. There is no sun." It was such a relief to give in and say it.

"There never was a *sun,*" said the Witch.

"No. There never was a sun," said the Prince, and the Marsh-wiggle, and the children.

For the last few minutes Jill had been feeling that there was something she must remember at all costs. And now she did. But it was dreadfully hard to say it. She felt as if huge weights were laid on her lips. At last, with an effort that seemed to take all the good out of her, she said:

"There's Aslan."

"Aslan?" said the Witch, quickening ever so slightly the pace of her thrumming. "What a pretty name! What does it mean?"

"He is the great Lion who called us out of our own world," said Scrubb, "and sent us into this to find Prince Rilian."

"What is a *lion*?" asked the Witch.

"Oh hang it all!" said Scrubb. "Don't you know? How can we describe it to her? Have you ever seen a cat?"

"Surely," said the Queen. "I love cats."

"Well a lion is a little bit—only a little bit, mind you —like a huge cat—with a mane. At least, it's not like a horse's mane, you know, it's more like a judge's wig. And it's yellow. And terrifically strong."

The Witch shook her head. "I see," she said, "that we should do no better with your *lion*, as you call it, than we did with your *sun*. You have seen lamps, and so you imagined a bigger and better lamp and called it the *sun*. You've seen cats, and now you want a bigger and better cat, and it's to so called a *lion*. Well, 'tis a pretty make-believe, though, to say truth, it would suit you all better if you were younger. And look how you can put nothing into your make-believe without copying it from the real world, this world of mine, which is the only world. But even you children are too old for such play. As for you, my lord Prince, that art a man full grown, fie upon you! Are you not ashamed of such toys? Come, all of you. Put away these childish tricks. I have work for you all in the real world. There is no Narnia, no Overworld, no sky, no sun, no Aslan. And now, to bed all. And let us begin a wiser life tomorrow. But first, to bed; to sleep; deep sleep, soft pillows, sleep without foolish dreams."

The Prince and the two children were standing with their heads hung down, their cheeks flushed, their eyes half closed; the strength all gone from them; the enchantment almost complete. But Puddleglum, desperately gathering all his strength, walked over to the fire. Then he did a very brave thing. He knew it wouldn't hurt him quite as much as it would hurt a human; for his feet (which were bare) were webbed and hard and cold-blooded like a duck's. But he knew it would hurt him badly enough; and so it did. With his bare foot he stamped on the fire, grinding a large part of it into ashes on the flat hearth. And three things happened at once.

First, the sweet heavy smell grew very much less. For though the whole fire had not been put out, a good bit of it had, and what remained smelled very largely of burnt Marsh-wiggle, which is not at all an enchanting smell. This instantly made everyone's brain far clearer. The Prince and the children held up their heads again and opened their eyes.

Secondly, the Witch, in a loud, terrible voice, utterly different from all the sweet tones she had been using up till now, called out, "What are you doing? Dare to touch my fire again, mud-filth, and I'll turn the blood to fire inside your veins."

Thirdly, the pain itself made Puddleglum's head for a moment perfectly clear and he knew exactly what he really thought. There is nothing like a good shock of pain for dissolving certain kinds of magic.

"One word, Ma'am," he said, coming back from the fire; limping, because of the pain. "One word. All you've been saying is quite right, I shouldn't wonder. I'm a chap who always liked to know the worst and then put the best face I can on it. So I won't deny any of what you said. But there's one thing more to be said, even so. Suppose we *have* only dreamed, or made up, all those things—trees and grass and sun and moon and stars and Aslan himself. Suppose we have. Then all I can say is that, in that case, the made-up things seem a good deal more important than the real ones. Suppose this black pit of a kingdom of yours *is* the only world. Well, it strikes me as a pretty poor one. And that's a funny thing, when you come to think of it. We're just babies making up a game, if you're right. But four babies playing a game can make a play-world which licks your real world hollow. That's why I'm going to stand by the play world. I'm on Aslan's side even if there isn't any Aslan to lead it. I'm going to live as like a Narnian as I can even if there isn't any Narnia. So, thanking you kindly for our supper, if these two gentlemen and the young lady are ready, we're leaving your court at once and setting out in the dark to spend our lives looking for Overland. Not that our lives will be very long, I should think; but that's small loss if the world's as dull a place as you say."

"Oh, hurrah! Good old Puddleglum!" cried Scrubb and Jill.

Meeting an Angel

Angels come from this "other world". Our world's literature and religion is full of angel stories. But few writers have described angels as creatively, convincingly, and compellingly as Lewis has, for example, in the following passage from *Perelandra*:

WE TEND TO THINK ABOUT non-human intelligences in two distinct categories which we label "scientific" and "supernatural" respectively. We think, in one mood, of Mr. Wells' Martians (very unlike the real Malacandrians, by the bye), or his Selenites. In quite a different mood we let our minds loose on the possibility of angels, ghosts, fairies, and the like. But the very moment we are compelled to recognise a creature in either class as *real* the distinction begins to get blurred: and when it is a creature like an eldil the distinction vanishes altogether. These things were not animals—to that extent one had to classify them with the second group; but they had some kind of material vehicle whose presence could (in principle) be scientifically verified. To that extent they belonged to the first group. The distinction between natural and supernatural, in fact, broke down; and when it had done so, one realised how great a comfort it had been—how it had eased the burden of intolerable strangeness which

Perelandra: A Novel (New York: Macmillan, 1952, 1961), pp. 17–18.

this universe imposes on us by dividing it into two halves and encouraging the mind never to think of both in the same context. What price we may have paid for this comfort in the way of false security and accepted confusion of thought is another matter. . . .

What I saw was simply a very faint rod or pillar of light. I don't think it made a circle of light either on the floor or the ceiling, but I am not sure of this. It certainly had very little power of illuminating its surroundings. So far, all is plain sailing. But it had two other characteristics which are less easy to grasp. One was its colour. Since I saw the thing I must obviously have seen it either white or coloured; but no efforts of my memory can conjure up the faintest image of what that colour was. I try blue, and gold, and violet, and red, but none of them will fit. How it is possible to have a visual experience which immediately and ever after becomes impossible to remember, I do not attempt to explain. The other was its angle. It was not at right angles to the floor. But as soon as I have said this, I hasten to add that this way of putting it is a later reconstruction. What one actually felt at the moment was that the column of light was vertical but the floor was not horizontal—the whole room seemed to have heeled over as if it were on board ship. The impression, however produced, was that this creature had reference to some horizontal, to some whole system of directions, based outside the Earth, and that its mere presence imposed that alien system on me and abolished the terrestrial horizontal.

I had no doubt at all that I was seeing an eldil, and little doubt that I was seeing the archon of Mars, the Oyarsa of Malacandra. And now that the thing had happened I was no longer in a condition of abject panic. My sensations were, it is true, in some ways very unpleasant. The fact that it was quite obviously not organic—the knowledge that intelligence was somehow located in this homogeneous cylinder of light but not related to it as our consciousness is related to our brains and nerves—was profoundly disturbing. It would not fit into our categories. The response which we ordinarily make to a living creature and that which we make to an inanimate object were here both equally inappropriate. On the other hand, all those doubts which I had felt before I entered the cottage as to whether these creatures were friend or foe, and whether Ransom were a pioneer or a dupe, had for the moment vanished. My fear was now of another kind. I felt sure that the creature was what we call "good," but I wasn't sure whether I liked "goodness" so much as I had supposed. This is a very terrible experience. As long as what you are afraid of is something evil, you may still hope that the good may come to your rescue. But suppose you struggle through to the good and find that it also is dreadful? How if food itself turns out to be the very thing you can't eat, and home the very place you can't live, and your very comforter the person who makes you uncomfortable? Then, indeed, there is no rescue possible: the last card has been played. For a second or two I was nearly in that condition. Here at last was a bit of that world from beyond the world, which I had always supposed that I loved and desired, breaking through and appearing to my senses: and I didn't like it, I wanted it to go away. I wanted every possible distance, gulf, curtain, blanket, and barrier to be placed between it and me.

"Allegory"

The following passage, from the beginning of *The Allegory of Love* (a scholarly book about medieval courtly love poetry) clearly distinguishes "allegory" and "symbolism" (which are often confused with each other). The view of this world as a "shadow-land" is an example of "symbolism", but it is a symbolism that is *discovered*, not *invented*. What is discovered is that this world is itself a symbol, sign, or shadow of another.

I T IS OF THE VERY NATURE of thought and language to represent what is immaterial in picturable terms. What is good or happy has always been high like the heavens and bright like the sun. Evil and misery were deep and dark from the first. . . . To ask how these married pairs of sensibles and insensibles first came together would be great folly; the real question is how they ever came apart. . . .

This fundamental equivalence between the immaterial and the material may be used by the mind in two ways. . . . On the one hand you can start with an immaterial fact, such as the passions which you actually experience, and can then invent *visibilia* to express them. . . . This is allegory. . . . But there is another way of using the equivalence, which is almost the opposite of allegory, and which I would call sacramentalism or symbolism. If our passions, being immaterial, can be copied by material inventions,

The Allegory of Love: A Study in Medieval Tradition (New York: Oxford University Press, 1958), pp. 44–46.

then it is possible that our material world in its turn is the copy of an invisible world. As the god Amor and his figurative garden are to the actual passions of men, so perhaps we ourselves and our 'real' world are to something else. The attempt to read that something else through its sensible imitations, to see the archetype in the copy, is what I mean by symbolism or sacramentalism. It is, in fine, 'the philosophy of Hermes that this visible world is but a picture of the invisible, wherein, as in a portrait, things are not truly but in equivocal shapes, as they counterfeit some real substance in that invisible fabrick'. The difference between the two can hardly be exaggerated. The allegorist leaves the given—his own passions—to talk of that which is confessedly less real, which is a fiction. The symbolist leaves the given to find that which is more real. To put the difference in another way, for the symbolist it is we who are the allegory. . . .

Symbolism comes to us from Greece. It makes its first effective appearance in European thought with the dialogues of Plato. The Sun is the copy of the Good. Time is the moving image of eternity. All visible things exist just in so far as they succeed in imitating the Forms.

"The Magician's Book"

Does it sometimes seem as if the most beautiful things you experience in this world are reminders of something even more beautiful?—like the magician's book in *The Voyage of the Dawn Treader*:

O N THE NEXT PAGE she came to a spell "for the refreshment of the spirit." The pictures were fewer here but very beautiful. And what Lucy found herself reading was more like a story than a spell. It went on for three pages and before she had read to the bottom of the page she had forgotten that she was reading at all. She was living in the story as if it were real, and all the pictures were real too. When she had got to the third page and come to the end, she said, "That is the loveliest story I've ever read or ever shall read in my whole life. Oh, I wish I could have gone on reading it for ten years. At least I'll read it over again."

But here part of the magic of the Book came into play. You couldn't turn back. The right-hand pages, the ones ahead, could be turned; the left hand pages could not.

"Oh, what a shame!" said Lucy. "I did so want to read it again. Well, at least, I must remember it. Let's see . . . it was about . . . about . . . oh dear, it's all fading away

The Voyage of the Dawn Treader (New York: Macmillan, 1952), pp. 130–31.

again. And even this last page is going blank. This is a very queer book. How can I have forgotten? It was about a cup and a sword and a tree and a green hill, I know that much. But I can't remember and what *shall* I do?"

And she never could remember; and ever since that day what Lucy means by a good story is a story which reminds her of the forgotten story in the Magician's Book.

❧❧

"Patches of Godlight"

If this whole world is a shadow, we want to run along the shadow to see the substance, the "more" that most people have called "God". Lewis offers us a way to adore God not by turning away from the world but by "looking along" it and seeing it as "patches of Godlight".

T HIS HEAVENLY FRUIT is instantly redolent of the orchard where it grew. This sweet air whispers of the country from whence it blows. It is a message. We know we are being touched by a finger of that right hand at which there are pleasures for evermore. There need be no question of thanks or praise as a separate event, something done afterwards. To experience the tiny theophany is itself to adore.

Gratitude exclaims, very properly, "How good of God to give me this." Adoration says, "What must be the quality of that Being whose far-off and momentary coruscations are like this!" One's mind runs back up the sunbeam to the sun. . . .

One must learn to walk before one can run. So here. We—or at least I—shall not be able to adore God on the highest occasions if we have learned no habit of doing so on the lowest. At best, our faith and reason will tell us that He is adorable, but we shall not have *found* Him so, not

Letters to Malcolm: Chiefly on Prayer (New York: Harcourt, Brace and World, 1963), pp. 90–91.

have "tasted and seen." Any patch of sunlight in a wood will show you something about the sun which you could never get from reading books on astronomy. These pure and spontaneous pleasures are "patches of Godlight" in the woods of our experience.

"Think of Yourself as a Seed"

Meanwhile, we are seeds waiting to bud, dreams waiting to waken.

T HINK OF YOURSELF just as a seed patiently waiting in the earth; waiting to come up a flower in the Gardener's good time, up into the *real* world, the real waking. I suppose that our whole present life, looked back on from there, will seem only a drowsy half-waking. We are here in the land of dreams. But cock-crow is coming. It is nearer now than when I began this letter.

Letters to an American Lady (Grand Rapids, Mich.: Wm. B. Eerdmans, 1967), p. 116.

II

JOY

"The most joy lies not in the having but in the desiring."

— *"Shadowlands"* (the movie)

The Mysterious Longing ("Joy")

MANY OF THE SHADOWS of this shadow-land are haunted—for instance, those shadows we call music, and the sea, and the eyes of your beloved, and the stars. We are drawn, not just *to* these things but *by* them, *through* them, to the unseen presence that haunts them, the "something more" that always eludes our definitions and escapes our conceptual cages that cannot confine it.

If there were another world beyond these shadow-lands and if we were made for it, then we would feel just such a longing for it, and a dissatisfaction with this world, even—especially —at its best, like an unconscious longing for land felt by a fish destined to evolve into an amphibian, or like an unborn baby's striving to be born. If God *had* made us for Himself, our hearts *would* be restless until they rest in Him.

No one since Augustine has written so movingly and memorably of this longing, C. S. Lewis' favorite theme. He calls it "Joy" and makes it the unifying theme of his autobiography, *Surprised by Joy*.

Two Mysteries of Desire

This desire is not clear but mysterious. But Lewis is clear *about* it, in defining the two ways this desire can be distinguished from every other, in the preface to his earliest prose book, *The Pilgrim's Regress: An Allegorical Apology for Christianity, Reason, and Romanticism.*

———————

THE EXPERIENCE is one of intense longing. It is distinguished from other longings by two things. In the first place, though the sense of want is acute and even painful, yet the mere wanting is felt to be somehow a delight. Other desires are felt as pleasures only if satisfaction is expected in the near future: hunger is pleasant only while we know (or believe) that we are soon going to eat. But this desire, even when there is no hope of possible satisfaction, continues to be prized, and even to be preferred to anything else in the world, by those who have once felt it. This hunger is better than any other fullness; this poverty better than all other wealth. And thus it comes about, that if the desire is long absent, it may itself be desired, and that new desiring becomes a new instance of the original desire, though the subject may not at once recognize the fact and thus cries out for his lost youth of soul at the very moment in which he is being rejuvenated.

From the Preface to *The Pilgrim's Regress: An Allegorical Apology for Christianity, Reason, and Romanticism* (Grand Rapids, Mich.: Wm. B. Eerdmans, 1943), pp. 7–10.

This sounds complicated, but it is simple when we live it. 'Oh to feel as I did then!' we cry; not noticing that even while we say the words the very feeling whose loss we lament is rising again in all its old bitter-sweetness. For this sweet Desire cuts across our ordinary distinctions between wanting and having. To have it is, by definition, a want: to want it, we find, is to have it.

In the second place, there is a peculiar mystery about the *object* of this Desire. Inexperienced people (and inattention leaves some inexperienced all their lives) suppose, when they feel it, that they know what they are desiring. Thus if it comes to a child while he is looking at a far off hillside he at once thinks 'if only I were there'; if it comes when he is remembering some event in the past, he thinks 'if only I could go back to those days'. If it comes (a little later) while he is reading a 'romantic' tale or poem of 'perilous seas and faerie lands forlorn', he thinks he is wishing that such places really existed and that he could reach them. If it comes (later still) in a context with erotic suggestions he believes he is desiring the perfect beloved. If he falls upon literature (like Maeterlinck or the early Yeats) which treats of spirits and the like with some show of serious belief, he may think that he is hankering for real magic and occultism. When it darts out upon him from his studies in history or science, he may confuse it with the intellectual craving for knowledge.

But every one of these impressions is wrong. The sole merit I claim for this book is that it is written by one who has proved them all to be wrong. There is no room for vanity in the claim: I know them to be wrong not by intelligence but by experience, such experience as would not have come my way if my youth had been wiser, more virtuous, and less self-centered than it was. For I have myself been deluded by every one of these false answers in turn, and have contemplated each of them earnestly enough to discover the cheat. To have embraced so many false Florimels is no matter for boasting: it is fools, they say, who learn by experience. But since they do at last learn, let a fool bring his experience into the common stock that wiser men may profit by it.

Every one of these supposed *objects* for the Desire is inadequate to it. An easy experiment will show that by going to the far hillside you will get either nothing, or else a recurrence of the same desire which sent you thither. A rather more difficult, but still possible, study of your own memories, will prove that by returning to the past you could not find, as a possession, that ecstasy which some sudden reminder of the past now moves you to desire. Those remembered moments were either quite commonplace at the time (and owe all their enchantment to memory) or else were themselves moments of desiring. . . . As for the sexual answer, that I suppose to be the most obviously false Florimel of all. On whatever plane you take it, it is not what we were looking for. Lust can be gratified. Another personality can become to us 'our America, our New-found-land'. A happy marriage can be achieved. But what has any of the three, or any mixture of the three, to do with that unnameable something, desire for which pierces us like a rapier at the smell of a bonfire, the sound of wild ducks flying overhead, the title of *The Well at the World's End,* the opening lines of *Kubla Khan,* the morning cobwebs in late summer, or the noise of falling waves?

It appeared to me therefore that if a man diligently followed this desire, pursuing the false objects until their falsity appeared and then resolutely abandoning them, he must come out at last into the clear knowledge that the human soul was made to enjoy some object that is never fully given—nay, cannot even be imagined as given—in our present mode of subjective and spatio-temporal experience. This Desire was, in the soul, as the Siege Perilous in Arthur's castle—the chair in which only one could sit. And if nature makes nothing in vain, the One who can sit in this chair must exist. I knew only too well how easily the longing accepts false objects and through what dark ways the pursuit of them leads us: but I also saw that the Desire itself contains the corrective of all these errors. The only fatal error was to pretend that you had passed from desire to fruition, when, in reality, you had found either nothing, or desire itself, or the satisfaction of some different desire. The dialectic of Desire, faithfully followed, would retrieve all mistakes, head you off from all false paths, and force you not to propound, but to live through, a sort of ontological proof.

Reading the Riddle,
Following the Clue

What follows are some of the essential passages from Lewis'
autobiography, *Surprised by Joy*. It is the story of how he followed the clue of this longing, like Ariadne's thread, until it
led him from atheism to God.

It begins with his three earliest childhood memories of
Joy:

T HE FIRST is itself the memory of a memory. As I
stood beside a flowering currant bush on a summer
day there suddenly arose in me without warning, and as if
from a depth not of years but of centuries, the memory of
that earlier morning at the Old House when my brother
had brought his toy garden into the nursery. It is difficult to find words strong enough for the sensation which
came over me; Milton's "enormous bliss" of Eden (giving
the full, ancient meaning to "enormous") comes somewhere near it. It was a sensation, of course, of desire; but
desire for what? not, certainly, for a biscuit tin filled with
moss, nor even (though that came into it) for my own
past. Ἰουλίανποθῶ [1]—and before I knew what I desired,
the desire itself was gone, the whole glimpse withdrawn,

Surprised by Joy: The Shape of My Early Life (New York: Harcourt,
Brace and World, 1955), pp. 16–18, 72–73, 75–77, 166, 168–70,
218–21, 180, 224–29, 237–38.

[1] Oh, I desire too much.

51

the world turned commonplace again, or only stirred by a longing for the longing that had just ceased. It had taken only a moment of time; and in a certain sense everything else that had ever happened to me was insignificant in comparison.

The second glimpse came through *Squirrel Nutkin*; through it only, though I loved all the Beatrix Potter books. But the rest of them were merely entertaining; it administered the shock, it was a trouble. It troubled me with what I can only describe as the Idea of Autumn. It sounds fantastic to say that one can be enamored of a season, but that is something like what happened; and, as before, the experience was one of intense desire. And one went back to the book, not to gratify the desire (that was impossible—how can one *possess* Autumn?) but to reawake it. And in this experience also there was the same surprise and the same sense of incalculable importance. It was something quite different from ordinary life and even from ordinary pleasure; something, as they would now say, "in another dimension."

The third glimpse came through poetry. I had become fond of Longfellow's *Saga of King Olaf*: fond of it in a casual, shallow way for its story and its vigorous rhythms. But then, and quite different from such pleasures, and like a voice from far more distant regions, there came a moment when I idly turned the pages of the book and found the unrhymed translation of *Tegner's Drapa* and read

> *I heard a voice that cried,*
> *Balder the beautiful*
> *Is dead, is dead—*

I knew nothing about Balder; but instantly I was uplifted into huge regions of northern sky, I desired with almost sickening intensity something never to be described (except that it is cold, spacious, severe, pale, and remote) and then, as in the other examples, found myself at the very same moment already falling out of that desire and wishing I were back in it.

The reader who finds these three episodes of no interest need read this book no further, for in a sense the central story of my life is about nothing else. For those who are still disposed to proceed I will only underline the quality common to the three experiences; it is that of an unsatisfied desire which is itself more desirable than any other satisfaction. I call it Joy, which is here a technical term and must be sharply distinguished both from Happiness and from Pleasure. Joy (in my sense) has indeed one characteristic, and one only, in common with them; the fact that anyone who has experienced it will want it again. Apart from that, and considered only in its quality, it might almost equally well be called a particular kind of unhappiness or grief. But then it is a kind we want. I doubt whether anyone who has tasted it would ever, if both were in his power, exchange it for all the pleasures in the world. But then Joy is never in our power and pleasure often is. . . .

Joy is distinct not only from pleasure in general but even from aesthetic pleasure. It must have the stab, the pang, the inconsolable longing. . . .

My eye fell upon a headline and a picture, carelessly, expecting nothing. A moment later, as the poet says, "The sky had turned round."

What I had read was the words *Siegfried and the Twilight of the Gods.* What I had seen was one of Arthur Rackham's illustrations to that volume. I had never heard of Wagner, nor of Siegfried. I thought the Twilight of the Gods meant the twilight in which the gods lived. How did I know, at once and beyond question, that this was no Celtic, or silvan, or terrestrial twilight? But so it was. Pure "Northernness" engulfed me: a vision of huge, clear spaces hanging above the Atlantic in the endless twilight of Northern summer, remoteness, severity . . . and almost at the same moment I knew that I had met this before, long, long ago (it hardly seems longer now) in *Tegner's Drapa,* that Siegfried (whatever it might be) belonged to the same world as Balder and the sunward-sailing cranes. And with that plunge back into my own past there arose at once, almost like heartbreak, the memory of Joy itself, the knowledge that I had once had what I had now lacked for years, that I was returning at last from exile and desert lands to my own country; and the distance of the Twilight of the Gods and the distance of my own past Joy, both unattainable, flowed together into a single, unendurable sense of desire and loss, which suddenly became one with the loss of the whole experience, which, as I now stared round that dusty schoolroom like a man recovering from unconsciousness, had already vanished, had eluded me at the very moment when I could first say *It is.* And at once I knew (with fatal knowledge) that to "have it

again" was the supreme and only important object of
desire. . . .

"Music" was one thing, "Wagnerian music" quite another, and there was no common measure between them;
it was not a new pleasure but a new kind of pleasure, if
indeed "pleasure" is the right word, rather than trouble,
ecstasy, astonishment, "a conflict of sensations without
name.". . .

✽✽

If the Northernness seemed then a bigger thing than my
religion, that may partly have been because my attitude
toward it contained elements which my religion ought
to have contained and did not. It was not itself a new
religion, for it contained no trace of belief and imposed
no duties. Yet unless I am greatly mistaken there was in
it something very like adoration, some kind of quite disinterested self-abandonment to an object which securely
claimed this by simply being the object it was. We are
taught in the Prayer Book to "give thanks to God for His
great glory," as if we owed Him more thanks for being
what He necessarily is than for any particular benefit He
confers upon us; and so indeed we do and to know God
is to know this. But I had been far from any such experience; I came far nearer to feeling this about the Norse
gods whom I disbelieved in than I had ever done about
the true God while I believed. Sometimes I can almost
think that I was sent back to the false gods there to ac-

quire some capacity for worship against the day when the true God should recall me to Himself. . . .

❦

It seemed to me that I had tasted heaven then. If only such a moment could return! But what I never realized was that it had returned—that the remembering of that walk was itself a new experience of just the same kind. True, it was desire, not possession. But then what I had felt on the walk had also been desire, and only possession in so far as that kind of desire is itself desirable, is the fullest possession we can know on earth; or rather, because the very nature of Joy makes nonsense of our common distinction between having and wanting. There, to have is to want and to want is to have. Thus, the very moment when I longed to be so stabbed again, was itself again such a stabbing. . . .

You will remember how, as a schoolboy, I had destroyed my religious life by a vicious subjectivism which made "realizations" the aim of prayer; turning away from God to seek states of mind, and trying to produce those states of mind by "maistry." With unbelievable folly I now proceeded to make exactly the same blunder in my imaginative life; or rather the same pair of blunders. The first was made at the very moment when I formulated the complaint that the "old thrill" was becoming rarer and rarer. For by that complaint I smuggled in the assumption that what I wanted was a "thrill," a state of my own mind. And there lies the deadly error. Only when your whole attention and desire are fixed on something else

—whether a distant mountain, or the past, or the gods of Asgard—does the "thrill" arise. It is a by-product. Its very existence presupposes that you desire not it but something other and outer. If by any perverse askesis or the use of any drug it could be produced from within, it would at once be seen to be of no value. For take away the object, and what, after all, would be left?—a whirl of images, a fluttering sensation in the diaphragm, a momentary abstraction. And who could want that? This, I say, is the first and deadly error, which appears on every level of life and is equally deadly on all, turning religion into a self-caressing luxury and love into auto-eroticism. And the second error is, having thus falsely made a state of mind your aim, to attempt to produce it. From the fading of the Northernness I ought to have drawn the conclusion that the Object, the Desirable, was further away, more external, less subjective, than even such a comparatively public and external thing as a system of mythology —had, in fact, only shone through that system. Instead, I concluded that it was a mood or state within myself which might turn up in any context. To "get it again" became my constant endeavor. . . .

❦

One thing, however, I learned, which has since saved me from many popular confusions of mind. I came to know by experience that it is not a disguise of sexual desire. Those who think that if adolescents were all provided with suitable mistresses we should soon hear no more of "immortal longings" are certainly wrong. I learned this mistake to be a mistake by the simple, if discreditable, process of repeatedly making it. . . . I repeatedly followed that path—to the end. And at the end one found pleasure; which immediately resulted in the discovery that pleasure (whether that pleasure or any other) was not what you had been looking for. No moral question was involved; I was at this time as nearly nonmoral on that subject as a human creature can be. The frustration did not consist in finding a "lower" pleasure instead of a "higher." It was the irrelevance of the conclusion that marred it. The hounds had changed scent. One had caught the wrong quarry. You might as well offer a mutton chop to a man who is dying of thirst as offer sexual pleasure to the desire I am speaking of. I did not recoil from the erotic conclusion with chaste horror, exclaiming, "Not that!" My feelings could rather have been expressed in the words, "Quite. I see. But haven't we wandered from the real point?" Joy is not a substitute for sex; sex is very often a substitute for Joy. I sometimes wonder whether all pleasures are not substitutes for Joy.

Such, then, was the state of my imaginative life; over against it stood the life of my intellect. The two hemispheres of my mind were in the sharpest contrast. On the one side a many-islanded sea of poetry and myth; on the other a glib and shallow "rationalism." Nearly all that I loved I believed to be imaginary; nearly all that I believed to be real I thought grim and meaningless. . . .

It seemed to me self-evident that one essential property of love, hate, fear, hope, or desire was attention to their object. To cease thinking about or attending to the woman is, so far, to cease loving; to cease thinking about or attending to the dreaded thing is, so far, to cease being afraid. But to attend to your own love or fear is to cease attending to the loved or dreaded object. . . . You cannot hope and also think about hoping at the same moment; for in hope we look to hope's object and we interrupt this by (so to speak) turning round to look at the hope itself. Of course the two activities can and do alternate with great rapidity; but they are distinct and incompatible. . . . This . . . could be verified in daily and hourly experience. The surest means of disarming an anger or a lust was to turn your attention from the girl or the insult and start examining the passion itself. The surest way of spoiling a pleasure was to start examining your satisfaction. But if so, it followed that all introspection is in one respect misleading. In introspection we try to look "inside ourselves" and see what is going on. But nearly everything that was going on a moment before is stopped by the very act of our turning to look at it. Unfortunately this does not mean that introspection finds nothing. On the contrary, it finds precisely what is left behind by the suspension of all our normal activities; and what is left behind is mainly mental images and physical sensations. The great error is to mistake this mere sediment or track or by-product for the activities themselves. That is how men may come to believe that thought is only unspoken words, or the appreciation of poetry only a collection of mental pictures. . . .

This discovery flashed a new light back on my whole life. I saw that all my waitings and watchings for Joy, all my vain hopes to find some mental content on which I could, so to speak, lay my finger and say, "This is it," had been a futile attempt. . . . I should never have to bother again about these images or sensations. I knew now that they were merely the mental track left by the passage of Joy—not the wave but the wave's imprint on the sand. The inherent dialectic of desire itself had in a way already shown me this; for all images and sensations, if idolatrously mistaken for Joy itself, soon honestly confessed themselves inadequate. All said, in the last resort, "It is not I. I am only a reminder. Look! Look! What do I remind you of?". . .

I had been equally wrong in supposing that I desired Joy itself. Joy itself, considered simply as an event in my own mind, turned out to be of no value at all. All the value lay in that of which Joy was the desiring. And that object, quite clearly, was no state of my own mind or body at all. . . . Inexorably Joy proclaimed, "You want —I myself am your want of—something other, outside, not you nor any state of you." I did not yet ask, Who is the desired? only What is it? But this brought me already into the region of awe, for I thus understood that in deepest solitude there is a road right out of the self, a commerce with something which, by refusing to identify itself with any object of the senses, or anything whereof we have biological or social need, or anything imagined, or any state of our own minds, proclaims itself sheerly objective. Far more objective than bodies, for it is not, like them, clothed in our senses; the naked Other, imageless (though our imagination salutes it with a hundred images), unknown, undefined, desired. . . .

It was as though the voice which had called to me from the world's end were now speaking at my side. It was with me in the room, or in my own body, or behind me. If it had once eluded me by its distance, it now eluded me by proximity—something too near to see, too plain to be understood, on this side of knowledge. It seemed to have been always with me; if I could ever have turned my head quick enough I should have seized it. Now for the first time I felt that it was out of reach not because of something I could not do but because of something I could not stop doing. If I could only leave off, let go, unmake myself, it would be there. . . .

I became aware that I was holding something at bay, or shutting something out. Or, if you like, that I was wearing some stiff clothing, like corsets, or even a suit of armor, as if I were a lobster. I felt myself being, there and then, given a free choice. I could open the door or keep it shut; I could unbuckle the armor or keep it on. Neither choice was presented as a duty; no threat or promise was attached to either, though I knew that to open the door or to take off the corslet meant the incalculable. The choice appeared to be momentous but it was also strangely unemotional. I was moved by no desires or fears. In a sense I was not moved by anything. I chose to open, to unbuckle, to loosen the rein. I say, "I chose," yet it did not really seem possible to do the opposite. On the other hand, I was aware of no motives. You could argue that I was not a free agent, but I am more inclined to think that this came nearer to being a perfectly free act than most that I have ever done. Necessity may not be the opposite of freedom, and perhaps a man is most free when, instead of producing motives, he could only say, "I am what I do." . . .

Really, a young Atheist cannot guard his faith too carefully. Dangers lie in wait for him on every side. . . . You must not do, you must not even try to do, the will of the Father unless you are prepared to "know of the doctrine." All my acts, desires, and thoughts were to be brought into harmony with universal Spirit. For the first time I examined myself with a seriously practical purpose. And there I found what appalled me; a zoo of lusts, a bedlam of ambitions, a nursery of fears, a harem of fondled hatreds. My name was legion.

Of course I could do nothing—I could not last out one hour—without continual conscious recourse to what I called Spirit. But the fine, philosophical distinction between this and what ordinary people call "prayer to God" breaks down as soon as you start doing it in earnest. Idealism can be talked, and even felt; it cannot be lived. It became patently absurd to go on thinking of "Spirit" as either ignorant of, or passive to, my approaches. Even if my own philosophy were true, how could the initiative lie on my side? My own analogy, as I now first perceived, suggested the opposite: if Shakespeare and Hamlet could ever meet, it must be Shakespeare's doing.[2] . . . The real terror was that if you seriously believed in even such a "God" or "Spirit" as I admitted, a wholly new situation

---

[2] *I.e.*, Shakespeare could, in principle, make himself appear as Author within the play, and write a dialogue between Hamlet and himself. The "Shakespeare" within the play would of course be at once Shakespeare and one of Shakespeare's creatures. It would bear some analogy to Incarnation.

developed. As the dry bones shook and came together in that dreadful valley of Ezekiel's, so now a philosophical theorem, cerebrally entertained, began to stir and heave and throw off its gravecloths, and stood upright and became a living presence. I was to be allowed to play at philosophy no longer. . . .

People who are naturally religious find difficulty in understanding the horror of such a revelation. Amiable agnostics will talk cheerfully about "man's search for God." To me, as I then was, they might as well have talked about the mouse's search for the cat. . . .

Remember, I had always wanted, above all things, not to be "interfered with." I had wanted (mad wish) "to call my soul my own." . . . Doubtless by definition, God was Reason itself. But would He also be "reasonable" in that other, more comfortable, sense? Not the slightest assurance on that score was offered me. Total surrender, the absolute leap in the dark, were demanded. The reality with which no treaty can be made was upon me. The demand was not even "All or nothing." . . . Now, the demand was simply "All."

You must picture me alone in that room in Magdalen, night after night, feeling, whenever my mind lifted even for a second from my work, the steady, unrelenting approach of Him whom I so earnestly desired not to meet. That which I greatly feared had at last come upon me. In the Trinity Term of 1929 I gave in, and admitted that God was God, and knelt and prayed: perhaps, that night, the most dejected and reluctant convert in all England. I did not then see what is now the most shining and obvious thing; the Divine humility which will accept a convert even on such terms. The Prodigal Son at least walked home on his own feet. But who can duly adore that Love which will open the high gates to a prodigal who is brought in kicking, struggling, resentful, and darting his eyes in every direction for a chance of escape? The words *compelle intrare*, compel them to come in, have been so abused by wicked men that we shudder at them; but, properly understood, they plumb the depth of the Divine mercy. The hardness of God is kinder than the softness of men, and His compulsion is our liberation. . . .

❧

Freedom, or necessity? Or do they differ at their maximum? At that maximum a man is what he does; there is nothing of him left over or outside the act. As for what we commonly call Will, and what we commonly call Emotion, I fancy these usually talk too loud, protest too much, to be quite believed, and we have a secret suspicion that the great passion or the iron resolution is partly a put-up job. . . .

But what, in conclusion, of Joy? for that, after all, is what the story has mainly been about. To tell you the truth, the subject has lost nearly all interest for me since I became a Christian. I cannot, indeed, complain, like Wordsworth, that the visionary gleam has passed away. I believe (if the thing were at all worth recording) that the old stab, the old bittersweet, has come to me as often and as sharply since my conversion as at any time of my life whatever. But I now know that the experience, considered as a state of my own mind, had never had the kind of importance I once gave it. It was valuable only as a pointer to something other and outer. While that other was in doubt, the pointer naturally loomed large in my thoughts. When we are lost in the woods the sight of a signpost is a great matter. He who first sees it cries, "Look!" The whole party gathers round and stares. But when we have found the road and are passing signposts every few miles, we shall not stop and stare. They will encourage us and we shall be grateful to the authority that set them up. But we shall not stop and stare, or not much; not on this road, though their pillars are of silver and their lettering of gold. "We would be at Jerusalem."

"Hope"

Lewis' *Mere Christianity* has remained for half a century probably the single most popular and convincing explanation of the fundamentals of the Faith. The following chapter shows how the longing we have explored above fits into and is explained by Christianity.

———————

HOPE IS ONE of the Theological virtues. This means that a continual looking forward to the eternal world is not (as some modern people think) a form of escapism or wishful thinking, but one of the things a Christian is meant to do. It does not mean that we are to leave the present world as it is. If you read history you will find that the Christians who did most for the present world were just those who thought most of the next. The Apostles themselves, who set on foot the conversion of the Roman Empire, the great men who built up the Middle Ages, the English Evangelicals who abolished the Slave Trade, all left their mark on Earth, precisely because their minds were occupied with Heaven. It is since Christians have largely ceased to think of the other world that they have become so ineffective in this. Aim at Heaven and you will get earth "thrown in": aim at earth and you will get neither. It seems a strange rule, but something like it can be seen at work in other matters. Health is a great

Mere Christianity (New York: Macmillan, 1952), pp. 118-21.

blessing, but the moment you make health one of your main, direct objects you start becoming a crank and imagining there is something wrong with you. You are only likely to get health provided you want other things more —food, games, work, fun, open air. In the same way, we shall never save civilisation as long as civilisation is our main object. We must learn to want something else even more.

Most of us find it very difficult to want "Heaven" at all—except in so far as "Heaven" means meeting again our friends who have died. One reason for this difficulty is that we have not been trained: our whole education tends to fix our minds on this world. Another reason is that when the real want for Heaven is present in us, we do not recognise it. Most people, if they had really learned to look into their own hearts, would know that they do want, and want acutely, something that cannot be had in this world. There are all sorts of things in this world that offer to give it to you, but they never quite keep their promise. The longings which arise in us when we first fall in love, or first think of some foreign country, or first take up some subject that excites us, are longings which no marriage, no travel, no learning, can really satisfy. I am not now speaking of what would be ordinarily called unsuccessful marriages, or holidays, or learned careers. I am speaking of the best possible ones. There was something we grasped at, in that first moment of longing, which just fades away in the reality. I think everyone knows what I mean. The wife may be a good wife, and the hotels and scenery may have been excellent, and chemistry may be a very interesting job: but something has evaded us. Now there are two wrong ways of dealing with this fact, and one right one.

(1) The Fool's Way—He puts the blame on the things themselves. He goes on all his life thinking that if only he tried another woman, or went for a more expensive holiday, or whatever it is, then, this time, he really would catch the mysterious something we are all after. Most of the bored, discontented, rich people in the world are of this type. They spend their whole lives trotting from woman to woman (through the divorce courts), from continent to continent, from hobby to hobby, always thinking that the latest is "the Real Thing" at last, and always disappointed.

(2) The Way of the Disillusioned "Sensible Man."—He soon decides that the whole thing was moonshine. "Of course," he says, "one feels like that when one's young. But by the time you get to my age you've given up chasing the rainbow's end." And so he settles down and learns not to expect too much and represses the part of himself which used, as he would say, "to cry for the moon." This is, of course, a much better way than the first, and makes a man much happier, and less of a nuisance to society. It tends to make him a prig (he is apt to be rather superior towards what he calls "adolescents"), but, on the whole, he rubs along fairly comfortably. It would be the best line we could take if man did not live for ever. But supposing infinite happiness really is there, waiting for us? Supposing one really can reach the rainbow's end? In that case it would be a pity to find out too late (a moment after death) that by our supposed "common sense" we had stifled in ourselves the faculty of enjoying it.

(3) The Christian Way.—The Christian says, "Creatures are not born with desires unless satisfaction for those desires exists. A baby feels hunger: well, there is such a thing as food. A duckling wants to swim: well, there is such a thing as water. Men feel sexual desire: well, there is such a thing as sex. If I find in myself a desire which no experience in this world can satisfy, the most probable explanation is that I was made for another world. If none of my earthly pleasures satisfy it, that does not prove that the universe is a fraud. Probably earthly pleasures were never meant to satisfy it, but only to arouse it, to suggest the real thing. If that is so, I must take care, on the one hand, never to despise, or be unthankful for, these earthly blessings, and on the other, never to mistake them for the something else of which they are only a kind of copy, or echo, or mirage. I must keep alive in myself the desire for my true country, which I shall not find till after death; I must never let it get snowed under or turned aside; I must make it the main object of life to press on to that other country and to help others to do the same."

There is no need to be worried by facetious people who try to make the Christian hope of "Heaven" ridiculous by saying they do not want "to spend eternity playing harps." The answer to such people is that if they cannot understand books written for grown-ups, they should not talk about them. All the scriptural imagery (harps, crowns, gold, etc.) is, of course, a merely symbolical attempt to express the inexpressible. Musical instruments are mentioned because for many people (not all) music is the thing known in the present life which most strongly suggests ecstasy and infinity. Crowns are mentioned to suggest the fact that those who are united with God in eternity share His splendour and power and joy. Gold is mentioned to suggest the timelessness of Heaven (gold does not rust) and the preciousness of it. People who take these symbols literally might as well think that when Christ told us to be like doves, He meant that we were to lay eggs.

"The Weight of Glory": Weaving the Spell of Good Magic

Next to the Narnia books, "The Weight of Glory" is probably the most well-loved thing Lewis ever wrote. It begins, in the following excerpt, with (1) a defense of desire, (2) a "good magic" spell to counter the evil spell of worldliness and materialism, and (3) an argument from the desire to the reality. The argument is the same as the one on page 69:

—If we have an innate, natural desire for X, there must be an X.
—We have an innate, natural desire for Heaven, for a greater world than these "shadow-lands".
—Therefore there must be a Heaven.

(This excerpt is from the beginning of "The Weight of Glory". The end can be found on pp. 83ff.)

I F THERE LURKS in most modern minds the notion that to desire our own good and earnestly to hope for the enjoyment of it is a bad thing, I submit that this notion has crept in from Kant and the Stoics and is no part of the Christian faith. Indeed, if we consider the unblushing promises of reward and the staggering nature of the rewards promised in the Gospels, it would seem that Our Lord finds our desires, not too strong, but too weak. We

"The Weight of Glory", in *The Weight of Glory and Other Addresses* (New York: Macmillan, 1949), pp. 1–2, 4–6.

are half-hearted creatures, fooling about with drink and sex and ambition when infinite joy is offered us, like an ignorant child who wants to go on making mud pies in a slum because he cannot imagine what is meant by the offer of a holiday at the sea. We are far too easily pleased.

We must not be troubled by unbelievers when they say that this promise of reward makes the Christian life a mercenary affair. There are different kinds of reward. There is the reward which has no natural connexion with the things you do to earn it, and is quite foreign to the desires that ought to accompany those things. Money is not the natural reward of love; that is why we call a man mercenary if he marries a woman for the sake of her money. But marriage is the proper reward for a real lover, and he is not mercenary for desiring it. A general who fights well in order to get a peerage is mercenary; a general who fights for victory is not, victory being the proper reward of battle as marriage is the proper reward of love. The proper rewards are not simply tacked on to the activity for which they are given, but are the activity itself in consummation. . . .

✤

In speaking of this desire for our own far-off country, which we find in ourselves even now, I feel a certain shyness. I am almost committing an indecency. I am trying to rip open the inconsolable secret in each one of you—the secret which hurts so much that you take your revenge on it by calling it names like Nostalgia and Romanticism and Adolescence; the secret also which pierces with such sweetness that when, in very intimate conversation, the mention of it becomes imminent, we grow awkward and affect to laugh at ourselves; the secret we cannot hide and cannot tell, though we desire to do both. We cannot tell it because it is a desire for something that has never actually appeared in our experience. We cannot hide it because our experience is constantly suggesting it, and we betray ourselves like lovers at the mention of a name. Our commonest expedient is to call it beauty and behave as if that had settled the matter. Wordsworth's expedient was to identify it with certain moments in his own past. But all this is a cheat. If Wordsworth had gone back to those moments in the past, he would not have found the thing itself, but only the reminder of it; what he remembered would turn out to be itself a remembering. The books or the music in which we thought the beauty was located will betray us if we trust to them; it was not *in* them, it only came *through* them, and what came through them was longing. These things—the beauty, the memory of our own past—are good images of what we really desire; but if they are mistaken for the thing itself they turn into dumb idols, breaking the hearts of their worshippers. For they are not the thing itself; they are only the scent of a flower we have not found, the echo of a tune we have not heard, news from a country we have never yet visited. Do you think I am trying to weave a spell? Perhaps I am; but remember your fairy tales. Spells are used for breaking enchantments as well as for inducing them. And you and I have need of the strongest spell that can be found to wake us from the evil enchantment of worldliness which has been laid upon us for nearly a hundred years. Almost our whole education has been directed to silencing this shy, persistent, inner voice; almost all our modern philosophies have been devised to convince us that the good of man is to be found on this earth. And yet it is a remarkable thing that such philosophies of Progress or Creative Evolution themselves bear reluctant witness to the truth that our real goal is elsewhere. When they want to convince you that earth is your home, notice how they set about it. They begin by trying to persuade you that earth can be made into heaven, thus giving a sop to your sense of exile in earth as it is. Next, they tell you that this fortunate event is still a good way off in the future, thus giving a sop to your knowledge that the fatherland is not here and now. Finally, lest your longing for the transtemporal should awake and spoil the whole affair, they use any rhetoric that comes to hand to keep out of your mind the recollection that even if all the happiness they promised could come to man on earth, yet still each generation would lose it by death, including the last generation of all, and the whole story would be nothing, not even a story, for ever and ever. . . .

Do what they will, then, we remain conscious of a desire which no natural happiness will satisfy. But is there any reason to suppose that reality offers any satisfaction to it? "Nor does the being hungry prove that we have bread." But I think it may be urged that this misses the point. A man's physical hunger does not prove that that man will get any bread; he may die of starvation on a raft in the Atlantic. But surely a man's hunger does prove that he comes of a race which repairs its body by eating and inhabits a world where eatable substances exist. In the same way, though I do not believe (I wish I did) that my desire for Paradise proves that I shall enjoy it, I think it a pretty good indication that such a thing exists and that some men will. A man may love a woman and not win her; but it would be very odd if the phenomenon called "falling in love" occurred in a sexless world.

Happiness, Not Unhappiness, Begets Longing

The desire arises not when we are miserable but when we are happy.

―――――――

"I HAVE ALWAYS—at least, ever since I can remember—had a kind of longing for death."

"Ah, Psyche," I said, "have I made you so little happy as that?"

"No, no, no," she said. "You don't understand. Not that kind of longing. It was when I was happiest that I longed most. It was on happy days when we were up there on the hills, the three of us, with the wind and the sunshine . . . where you couldn't see Glome or the palace. Do you remember? The colour and the smell, and looking across at the Grey Mountain in the distance? And because it was so beautiful, it set me longing, always longing. Somewhere else there must be more of it. Everything seemed to be saying, Psyche come! But I couldn't (not yet) come and I didn't know where I was to come to. It almost hurt me. I felt like a bird in a cage when the other birds of its kind are flying home."

Till We Have Faces: A Myth Retold (New York: Harcourt Brace and Company, 1956), p. 74.

The Preciousness of Longing

Eliciting this desire is one of the highest functions of human art.

H AVE YOU NOT SEEN that in our days
Of any whose story, song, or art
Delights us, our sincerest praise
Means, when all's said, 'You break my heart'?[1]

❦

Why should I leave this green-floored cell,
Roofed with blue air, in which we dwell,
Unless, outside its guarded gates,
Long, long desired, the Unearthly waits,
Strangeness that moves us more than fear,
Beauty that stabs with tingling spear,
Or Wonder, laying on one's heart
That finger-tip at which we start
As if some thought too swift and shy
For reason's grasp had just gone by?[2]

[1] "Epigrams and Epitaphs", no. 2 from *Poems*, edited by Walter Hooper (New York: Harcourt, Brace and World, 1964), p. 133.
[2] "An Expostulation" from *Poems*, p. 58.

III

HEAVEN

"Real life hasn't begun yet."
"Jack, you'd better be right."

— *"Shadowlands"* (the movie)

"The Land from Which the Shadows Fall" (Heaven)

C. S. LEWIS OFTEN WONDERED what it would be like to attain this "unattainable ecstasy". Of course, no one can define it: "Eye has not seen, ear has not heard, nor has it entered into the heart of man, the things God has prepared for those who love him." But our lives breathe heavy with hints and suggestions, with "the weight of glory".

Our conventional pictures of Heaven—clouds, harps, haloes, cherubs—do not *move* us. Here are some moving pictures.

"Immortal Horrors or Everlasting Splendours"

The last paragraph of "The Weight of Glory" focuses on the weightiest of all earth's reminders of Heaven: Heaven's citizens, our neighbors. The last paragraph does nothing less than give us a vision of the meaning of our lives than which there is simply none greater.

———————

WE ARE TO SHINE AS THE SUN, we are to be given the Morning Star. I think I begin to see what it means. In one way, of course, God has given us the Morning Star already: you can go and enjoy the gift on many fine mornings if you get up early enough. What more, you may ask, do we want? Ah, but we want so much more—something the books on aesthetics take little notice of. But the poets and the mythologies know all about it. We do not want merely to *see* beauty, though, God knows, even that is bounty enough. We want something else which can hardly be put into words—to be united with the beauty we see, to pass into it, to receive it into ourselves, to bathe in it, to become part of it. That is why we have peopled air and earth and water with gods and goddesses and nymphs and elves—that, though we cannot, yet these projections can, enjoy in themselves that beauty, grace, and power of which Nature is the image. That is why the poets tell us

"The Weight of Glory", pp. 12–15.

such lovely falsehoods. They talk as if the west wind could really sweep into a human soul; but it can't. They tell us that "beauty born of murmuring sound" will pass into a human face; but it won't. Or not yet. For if we take the imagery of Scripture seriously, if we believe that God will one day *give* us the Morning Star and cause us to *put on* the splendour of the sun, then we may surmise that both the ancient myths and the modern poetry, so false as history, may be very near the truth as prophecy. At present we are on the outside of the world, the wrong side of the door. We discern the freshness and purity of morning, but they do not make us fresh and pure. We cannot mingle with the splendours we see. But all the leaves of the New Testament are rustling with the rumour that it will not always be so. Some day, God willing, we shall get *in*. When human souls have become as perfect in voluntary obedience as the inanimate creation is in its lifeless obedience, then they will put on its glory, or rather that greater glory of which Nature is only the first sketch. For you must not think that I am putting forward any heathen fancy of being absorbed into Nature. Nature is mortal; we shall outlive her. When all the suns and nebulae have passed away, each one of you will still be alive. Nature is only the image, the symbol; but it is the symbol Scripture invites me to use. We are summoned to pass in through Nature, beyond her, into that splendour which she fitfully reflects.

And in there, in beyond Nature, we shall eat of the tree of life. At present, if we are reborn in Christ, the spirit in us lives directly on God; but the mind, and still more the body, receives life from Him at a thousand removes —through our ancestors, through our food, through the elements. The faint, far-off results of those energies which God's creative rapture implanted in matter when He made the worlds are what we now call physical pleasures; and even thus filtered, they are too much for our present management. What would it be to taste at the fountain-head that stream of which even these lower reaches prove so intoxicating? Yet that, I believe, is what lies before us. The whole man is to drink joy from the fountain of joy. As St. Augustine said, the rapture of the saved soul will "flow over" into the glorified body. In the light of our present specialized and depraved appetites we cannot imagine this *torrens voluptatis*, and I warn everyone most seriously not to try. But it must be mentioned, to drive out thoughts even more misleading—thoughts that what is saved is a mere ghost, or that the risen body lives in numb insensibility. The body was made for the Lord, and these dismal fancies are wide of the mark.

Meanwhile the cross comes before the crown and to-morrow is a Monday morning. A cleft has opened in the pitiless walls of the world, and we are invited to follow our great Captain inside. The following Him is, of course, the essential point. That being so, it may be asked what practical use there is in the speculations which I have been indulging. I can think of at least one such use. It may be possible for each to think too much of his own potential glory hereafter; it is hardly possible for him to think too often or too deeply about that of his neighbour. The load, or weight, or burden of my neighbour's glory should be laid daily on my back, a load so heavy that only humility can carry it, and the backs of the proud will be broken. It is a serious thing to live in a society of possible gods and goddesses, to remember that the dullest and most uninteresting person you talk to may one day be a creature which, if you saw it now, you would be strongly tempted to worship, or else a horror and a corruption such as you now meet, if at all, only in a nightmare. All day long we are, in some degree, helping each other to one or other of these destinations. It is in the light of these overwhelming possibilities, it is with the awe and the circumspection proper to them, that we should conduct all our dealings with one another, all friendships, all loves, all play, all politics. There are no *ordinary* people. You have never talked to a mere mortal. Nations, cultures, arts, civilization—these are mortal, and their life is to ours as the life of a gnat. But it is immortals whom we joke with, work with, marry, snub, and exploit—immortal horrors or everlasting splendours. This does not mean that we are to be perpetually solemn. We must play. But our merriment must be of that kind (and it is, in fact, the merriest kind) which exists between people who have, from the outset, taken each other seriously—no flippancy, no superiority, no presumption. And our charity must be a real and costly love, with deep feeling for the sins in spite of which we love the sinner—no mere tolerance or indulgence which parodies love as flippancy parodies merriment. Next to the Blessed Sacrament itself, your neighbour is the holiest object presented to your senses. If he is your Christian neighbour he is holy in almost the same way, for in him also Christ *vere latitat* —the glorifier and the glorified, Glory Himself, is truly hidden.

"Man or Rabbit?"

Heaven's life is more than morality.

MERE *MORALITY* is not the end of life. You were made for something quite different from that. J. S. Mill and Confucius (Socrates was much nearer the reality) simply didn't know what life is about. The people who keep on asking if they can't lead a decent life without Christ, don't know what life is about; if they did they would know that "a decent life" is mere machinery compared with the thing we men are really made for. Morality is indispensable: but the Divine Life, which gives itself to us and which calls us to be gods, intends for us something in which morality will be swallowed up. We are to be remade. All the rabbit in us is to disappear—the worried, conscientious, ethical rabbit as well as the cowardly and sensual rabbit. We shall bleed and squeal as the handfuls of fur come out; and then, surprisingly, we shall find underneath it all a thing we have never yet imagined: a real Man, an ageless god, a son of God, strong, radiant, wise, beautiful, and drenched in joy.

God in the Dock, p. 112.

Is Heaven Playful or Serious?

Is Heaven playful or serious? Both! It triumphantly solves this earthly dilemma. (Lewis himself had the ability, unusual in our grim and shallow times, to be neither grim nor shallow but joyful and serious at the same time—a foretaste of Heaven.)

I KNOW THAT MY TENDENCY to use images like play and dance for the highest things is a stumbling-block to you. You . . . call it "heartless." you feel it a brutal mockery of every martyr and every slave that a world-process which is so desperately serious to the actors should, at whatever celestial apex, be seen in terms of frivolities. And you add that it comes with a ludicrously ill grace from me, who never enjoyed any game and can dance no better than a centipede with wooden legs. But I still think you don't see the real point.

I do *not* think that the life of Heaven bears any analogy to play or dance in respect of frivolity. I do think that while we are in this "valley of tears," cursed with labour, hemmed round with necessities, tripped up with frustrations, doomed to perpetual plannings, puzzlings, and anxieties, certain qualities that must belong to the celestial condition have no chance to get through, can project no image of themselves, except in activities which, for us here and now, are frivolous. For surely we must suppose

Letters to Malcolm, pp. 92–93.

the life of the blessed to be an end in itself, indeed The End: to be utterly spontaneous; to be the complete reconciliation of boundless freedom with order—with the most delicately adjusted, supple, intricate, and beautiful order? How can you find any image of this in the "serious" activities either of our natural or of our (present) spiritual life? Either in our precarious and heartbroken affections or in the Way which is always, in some degree, a *via crucis*? No, Malcolm. It is only in our "hours-off," only in our moments of permitted festivity, that we find an analogy. Dance and game *are* frivolous, unimportant down here; for "down here" is not their natural place. Here, they are a moment's rest from the life we were placed here to live. But in this world everything is upside down. That which, if it could be prolonged here, would be a truancy, is likest that which in a better country is the End of ends. Joy is the serious business of Heaven.

A Modern Mini-*Divine Comedy*

The Great Divorce is a modern mini-version of Dante's *Divine Comedy*: a fantasy about a bus trip from Hell to Purgatory and Heaven.

The Preface opposes the traditional worldview, with a real Heaven and Hell, to the modern one:

BLAKE WROTE the Marriage of Heaven and Hell. If I have written of their Divorce, this is not because I think myself a fit antagonist for so great a genius, nor even because I feel at all sure that I know what he meant. But in some sense or other the attempt to make that marriage is perennial. The attempt is based on the belief that reality never presents us with an absolutely unavoidable "either-or", that, granted skill and patience and (above all) time enough, some way of embracing both alternatives can always be found; that mere development or adjustment or refinement will somehow turn evil into good without our being called on for a final and total rejection of anything we should like to retain. This belief I take to be a disastrous error. You cannot take all luggage with you on all journeys; on one journey even your right hand and your right eye may be among the things you have to leave behind. We are not living in a world where all roads are radii of a circle and where all, if followed long

The Great Divorce (New York: Macmillan, 1946), pp. v–vii.

enough, will therefore draw gradually nearer and finally
meet at the centre: rather in a world where every road,
after a few miles, forks into two, and each of those into
two again, and at each fork you must make a decision.
Even on the biological level life is not like a pool but like
a tree. It does not move towards unity but away from it
and the creatures grow further apart as they increase in
perfection. Good, as it ripens, becomes continually more
different not only from evil but from other good.

I do not think that all who choose wrong roads perish;
but their rescue consists in being put back on the right
road. A wrong sum can be put right: but only by going
back till you find the error and working it afresh from
that point, never by simply *going on*. Evil can be undone,
but it cannot "develop" into good. Time does not heal
it. The spell must be unwound, bit by bit, "with back-
ward mutters of dissevering power"—or else not. It is
still "either-or." If we insist on keeping Hell (or even
earth) we shall not see Heaven: if we accept Heaven we
shall not be able to retain even the smallest and most intimate souvenirs of Hell. I believe, to be sure, that any
man who reaches Heaven will find that what he aban-
doned (even in plucking out his right eye) was precisely
nothing: that the kernel of what he was really seeking even
in his most depraved wishes will be there, beyond expec-
tation, waiting for him in "the High Countries." In that
sense it will be true for those who have completed the
journey (and for no others) to say that good is everything
and Heaven everywhere. But we, at this end of the road,
must not try to anticipate that retrospective vision. If we
do, we are likely to embrace the false and disastrous con-

verse and fancy that everything is good and everywhere is Heaven.

But what, you ask, of earth? Earth, I think, will not be found by anyone to be in the end a very distinct place. I think earth, if chosen instead of Heaven, will turn out to have been, all along, only a region in Hell: and earth, if put second to Heaven, to have been from the beginning a part of Heaven itself.

In the following passage from *The Great Divorce*, George Mac-Donald, who appears as Lewis' Vergil to guide him, explains how "all that seems earth is Hell or Heaven" (as Lewis put it elsewhere):

———————

"BOTH GOOD AND EVIL, when they are full grown, become retrospective. Not only this valley but all this earthly past will have been Heaven to those who are saved. Not only the twilight in that town, but all their life on earth too, will then be seen by the damned to have been Hell. That is what mortals misunderstand. They say of some temporal suffering, 'No future bliss can make up for it,' not knowing that Heaven, once attained, will work backwards and turn even that agony into a glory. And of some sinful pleasure they say 'Let me but have *this* and I'll take the consequences': little dreaming how damnation

The Great Divorce, pp. 67–69.

will spread back and back into their past and contaminate the pleasure of the sin. Both processes begin even before death. The good man's past begins to change so that his forgiven sins and remembered sorrows take on the quality of Heaven: the bad man's past already conforms to his badness and is filled only with dreariness. And that is why, at the end of all things, when the sun rises here and the twilight turns to blackness down there, the Blessed will say, 'We have never lived anywhere except in Heaven,' and the Lost, 'We were always in Hell.' And both will speak truly." . . .

"Then those people are right who say that Heaven and Hell are only states of mind?"

"Hush," said he sternly. "Do not blaspheme. Hell is a state of mind—ye never said a truer word. And every state of mind, left to itself, every shutting up of the creature within the dungeon of its own mind—is, in the end, Hell. But Heaven is not a state of mind. Heaven is reality itself. All that is fully real is Heavenly. For all that can be shaken will be shaken and only the unshakable remains."

"Further Up and Further In"

What George MacDonald the guide told Lewis the narrator in the previous passage, from *The Great Divorce*, about the close connection between earth and Heaven, Lewis now portrays concretely at the very end of the Chronicles of Narnia, in *The Last Battle*. Put boldly, it is a story for children about the end of the world. The characters are entering Heaven, and Lewis dares to imagine what they find.

―――――――――

THEN THEY ALL WENT FORWARD TOGETHER, always westward, for that seemed to be the direction Aslan had meant when he cried out "Further up and further in." Many other creatures were slowly moving the same way, but that grassy country was very wide and there was no crowding.

It still seemed to be early and the morning freshness was in the air. They kept on stopping to look round and to look behind them, partly because it was so beautiful but partly also because there was something about it which they could not understand.

"Peter," said Lucy, "where is this, do you suppose?"

"I don't know," said the High King. "It reminds me of somewhere but I can't give it a name. Could it be somewhere we once stayed for a holiday when we were very, very small?"

The Last Battle (New York: Macmillan, 1956), pp. 158–62.

"It would have to have been a jolly good holiday," said Eustace. "I bet there isn't a country like this anywhere in *our* world. Look at the colours? You couldn't get a blue like the blue on those mountains in our world."

"Is it not Aslan's country?" said Tirian.

"Not like Aslan's country on top of that mountain beyond the eastern end of the world," said Jill. "I've been there."

"If you ask me," said Edmund, "It's like somewhere in the Narnian world. Look at those mountains ahead—and the big ice-mountains beyond them. Surely they're rather like the mountains we used to see from Narnia, the ones up Westward beyond the Waterfall?"

"Yes, so they are," said Peter. "Only these are bigger."

"I don't think *those* ones are so very like anything in Narnia," said Lucy. "But look there." She pointed southward to their left, and everyone stopped and turned to look. "Those hills," said Lucy, "the nice woody ones and the blue ones behind—aren't they very like the southern border of Narnia?"

"Like!" cried Edmund after a moment's silence. "Why they're exactly like. Look, there's Mount Pire with his forked head, and there's the pass into Archenland and everything!"

"And yet they're not like," said Lucy. "They're different. They have more colours on them and they look further away than I remembered and they're more . . . more . . . oh, I don't know. . . ."

"More like the real thing," said the Lord Digory softly. Suddenly Farsight the Eagle spread his wings, soared thirty or forty feet up into the air, circled round and then alighted on the ground.

"Kings and Queens," he cried, "we have all been blind. We are only beginning to see where we are. From up there I have seen it all—Ettinsmuir, Beaversdam, the Great River, and Cair Paravel still shining on the edge of the Eastern Sea. Narnia is not dead. This is Narnia."

"But how can it be?" said Peter. "For Aslan told us older ones that we should never return to Narnia, and here we are."

"Yes," said Eustace. "And we saw it all destroyed and the sun put out."

"And it's all so different," said Lucy.

"The Eagle is right," said the Lord Digory. "Listen, Peter. When Aslan said you could never go back to Narnia, he meant the Narnia you were thinking of. But that was not the real Narnia. That had a beginning and an end. It was only a shadow or a copy of the real Narnia, which has always been here and always will be here: just as our own world, England and all, is only a shadow or copy of something in Aslan's real world. You need not mourn over Narnia, Lucy. All of the old Narnia that mattered, all the dear creatures, have been drawn into the real Narnia through the Door. And of course it is different; as different as a real thing is from a shadow or as waking life is from a dream." His voice stirred everyone like a trumpet as he spoke these words: but when he added under his breath "It's all in Plato, all in Plato: bless me, what *do* they teach them at these schools!" the older ones laughed. It was so exactly like the sort of thing they had heard him say long ago in that other world where his beard was grey instead of golden. He knew why they were laughing and joined in the laugh himself. But very quickly they all became grave again: for, as you know, there is a kind of happiness and wonder that makes you serious. It is too good to waste on jokes.

It is as hard to explain how this sunlit land was different from the old Narnia, as it would be to tell you how the fruits of that country taste. Perhaps you will get some idea of it, if you think like this. You may have been in a room in which there was a window that looked out on a lovely bay of the sea or a green valley that wound away among mountains. And in the wall of that room opposite to the window there may have been a looking glass. And as you turned away from the window you suddenly caught sight of that sea or that valley, all over again, in the looking glass. And the sea in the mirror, or the valley in the mirror, were in one sense just the same as the real ones: yet at the same time they were somehow different—deeper, more wonderful, more like places in a story: in a story you have never heard but very much want to know. The difference between the old Narnia and the new Narnia was like that. The new one was a deeper country: every rock and flower and blade of grass looked as if it meant more. I can't describe it any better than that: if you ever get there, you will know what I mean.

It was the Unicorn who summed up what everyone was feeling. He stamped his right fore-hoof on the ground and neighed and then cried:

"I have come home at last! This is my real country! I belong here. This is the land I have been looking for all my life, though I never knew it till now. The reason why we loved the old Narnia is that it sometimes looked a little like this. Bree-hee-hee! Come further up, come further in!"

"Farewell to Shadow-Lands"

ABOUT HALF AN HOUR LATER—or it might have been half a hundred years later, for time there is not like time here—Lucy stood with her dear friend, her oldest Narnian friend, the Faun Tumnus, looking down over the wall of that garden, and seeing all Narnia spread out below. But when you looked down you found that this hill was much higher than you had thought: it sank down with shining cliffs, thousands of feet below them and trees in that lower world looked no bigger than grains of green salt. Then she turned inward again and stood with her back to the wall and looked at the garden.

"I see," she said at last, thoughtfully. "I see now. This garden is like the Stable. It is far bigger inside than it was outside."

"Of course, Daughter of Eve," said the Faun. "The further up and the further in you go, the bigger everything gets. The inside is larger than the outside."

Lucy looked hard at the garden and saw that it was not really a garden at all but a whole world, with its own rivers and woods and sea and mountains. But they were not strange: she knew them all.

"I see," she said. "This is still Narnia, and, more real and more beautiful than the Narnia down below, just as *it* was more real and more beautiful than the Narnia outside the Stable door! I see . . . world within world, Narnia within Narnia. . . ."

The Last Battle, pp. 170–74.

"Yes," said Mr. Tumnus, "like an onion: except that as you continue to go in and in, each circle is larger than the last."

And Lucy looked this way and that and soon found that a new and beautiful thing had happened to her. Whatever she looked at, however far away it might be, once she had fixed her eyes steadily on it, became quite clear and close as if she were looking through a telescope. She could see the whole southern desert and beyond it the great city of Tashbaan: to eastward she could see Cair Paravel on the edge of the sea and the very window of the room that had once been her own. And far out to sea she could discover the islands, island after island to the end of the world, and, beyond the end, the huge mountain which they had called Aslan's country. But now she saw that it was part of a great chain of mountains which ringed round the whole world. In front of her it seemed to come quite close. Then she looked to her left and saw what she took to be a great bank of brightly-coloured cloud, cut off from them by a gap. But she looked harder and saw that it was not a cloud at all but a real land. And when she had fixed her eyes on one particular spot of it, she at once cried out, "Peter! Edmund! Come and look! Come quickly." And they came and looked, for their eyes also had become like hers.

"Why!" exclaimed Peter. "It's England. And that's the house itself—Professor Kirk's old home in the country where all our adventures began!"

"I thought that house had been destroyed," said Edmund.

"So it was," said the Faun. "But you are now looking

at the England within England, the real England just as this is the real Narnia. And in that inner England no good thing is destroyed."

Suddenly they shifted their eyes to another spot, and then Peter and Edmund and Lucy gasped with amazement and shouted out and began waving: for there they saw their own father and mother, waving back at them across the great, deep valley. It was like when you see people waving at you from the deck of a big ship when you are waiting on the quay to meet them.

"How can we get at them?" said Lucy.

"That is easy," said Mr. Tumnus. "That country and this country—all the *real* countries—are only spurs jutting out from the great mountains of Aslan. We have only to walk along the ridge, upward and inward, till it joins on. And listen! There is King Frank's horn: we must all go up."

And soon they found themselves all walking together—and a great, bright procession it was—up towards mountains higher than you could see in this world even if they were there to be seen. But there was no snow on those mountains: there were forests and green slopes and sweet orchards and flashing waterfalls, one above the other, going up for ever. And the land they were walking on grew narrower all the time, with a deep valley on each side: and across that valley the land which was the real England grew nearer and nearer.

The light ahead was growing stronger. Lucy saw that a great series of many-coloured cliffs led up in front of them like a giant's staircase. And then she forgot everything else, because Aslan himself was coming, leaping down from cliff to cliff like a living cataract of power and beauty.

And the very first person whom Aslan called to him was Puzzle the Donkey. You never saw a donkey look feebler and sillier than Puzzle did as he walked up to Aslan; and he looked, beside Aslan, as small as a kitten looks beside a St. Bernard. The Lion bowed down his head and whispered something to Puzzle at which his long ears went down; but then he said something else at which the ears perked up again. The humans couldn't hear what he had said either time. Then Aslan turned to them and said:

"You do not yet look so happy as I mean you to be."

Lucy said, "We're so afraid of being sent away, Aslan. And you have sent us back into our own world so often."

"No fear of that," said Aslan. "Have you not guessed?"

Their hearts leaped and a wild hope rose within them.

"There *was* a real railway accident," said Aslan softly. "Your father and mother and all of you are—as you used to call it in the Shadow-Lands—dead. The term is over: the holidays have begun. The dream is ended: this is the morning."

And as He spoke He no longer looked to them like a lion; but the things that began to happen after that were so great and beautiful that I cannot write them. And for us this is the end of all the stories, and we can most truly say that they all lived happily ever after. But for them it was only the beginning of the real story. All their life in this world and all their adventures in Narnia had only been the cover and the title page: now at last they were beginning Chapter One of the Great Story, which no one on earth has read: which goes on for ever: in which every chapter is better than the one before.

"Heaven"

If you got the impression from the movie that Lewis' earlier theology was simplistic and cliché-ridden, the following excerpt will dispel that illusion. It is the conclusion of *The Problem of Pain*. (The rest of the book is summarized on pp. 177–89.) It is a daringly creative yet totally orthodox treatise on Heaven. *This*, according to Lewis, is what all Joy points to and what all suffering, like labor pains, finally gives birth to.

Theologians and philosophers have written brilliant and profound things about Heaven, but I think you have to be also a saint to write this chapter.

It is not an *easy* read—not because of style but because of content—and demands more than one reading. Each phrase deserves and rewards meditation. It brings us "further up and further in" than *The Last Battle* brought us. Indeed, it can be seen as an "unpacking" of the last line of that book (see pp. 102–3).

"I RECKON", said St Paul, "that the sufferings of this present time are not worthy to be compared with the glory that shall be revealed in us." If this is so, a book on suffering which says nothing of heaven, is leaving out almost the whole of one side of the account. Scripture and tradition habitually put the joys of heaven into the scale against the sufferings of earth, and no solution of the prob-

The Problem of Pain (Glasgow: William Collins and Company, 1949), pp. 115–23.

lem of pain which does not do so can be called a Christian one. We are very shy nowadays of even mentioning heaven. We are afraid of the jeer about "pie in the sky", and of being told that we are trying to "escape" from the duty of making a happy world here and now into dreams of a happy world elsewhere. But either there is "pie in the sky" or there is not. If there is not, then Christianity is false, for the doctrine is woven into its whole fabric. If there is, then this truth, like any other, must be faced, whether it is useful at political meetings or no. Again, we are afraid that heaven is a bribe, and that if we make it our goal we shall no longer be disinterested. It is not so. Heaven offers nothing that a mercenary soul can desire. It is safe to tell the pure in heart that they shall see God, for only the pure in heart want to. There are rewards that do not sully motives. A man's love for a woman is not mercenary because he wants to marry her, nor his love for poetry mercenary because he wants to read it, nor his love of exercise less disinterested because he wants to run and leap and walk. Love, by definition, seeks to enjoy its object.

You may think that there is another reason for our silence about heaven—namely, that we do not really desire it. But that may be an illusion. What I am now going to say is merely an opinion of my own without the slightest authority, which I submit to the judgement of better Christians and better scholars than myself. There have been times when I think we do not desire heaven; but more often I find myself wondering whether, in our heart of hearts, we have ever desired anything else. You may have noticed that the books you really love are bound together by a secret thread. You know very well what is the common quality that makes you love them, though you cannot put it into words: but most of your friends do not see it at all, and often wonder why, liking this, you should also like that. Again, you have stood before some landscape, which seems to embody what you have been looking for all your life; and then turned to the friend at your side who appears to be seeing what you saw—but at the first words a gulf yawns between you, and you realise that this landscape means something totally different to him, that he is pursuing an alien vision and cares nothing for the ineffable suggestion by which you are transported. Even in your hobbies, has there not always been some secret attraction which the others are curiously ignorant of —something, not to be identified with, but always on the verge of breaking through, the smell of cut wood in the workshop or the clap-clap of water against the boat's side? Are not all lifelong friendships born at the moment when at last you meet another human being who has some inkling (but faint and uncertain even in the best) of that something which you were born desiring, and which, beneath the flux of other desires and in all the momentary silences between the louder passions, night and day, year by year, from childhood to old age, you are looking for, watching for, listening for? You have never *had* it. All the things that have ever deeply possessed your soul have been but hints of it—tantalising glimpses, promises never quite fulfilled, echoes that died away just as they caught your ear. But if it should really become manifest—if there ever came an echo that did not die away but swelled into the sound itself—you would know it. Beyond all possibility of doubt you would say "Here at last is the thing I was made for". We cannot tell each other about it. It is the secret signature of each soul, the incommunicable and unappeasable want, the thing we desired before we met our wives or made our friends or chose our work, and which we shall still desire on our deathbeds, when the mind no longer knows wife or friend or work. While we are, this is. If we lose this, we lose all.

This signature on each soul may be a product of heredity and environment, but that only means that heredity and environment are among the instruments whereby God creates a soul. I am considering not how, but why, He makes each soul unique. If He had no use for all these differences, I do not see why He should have created more souls than one. Be sure that the ins and outs of your individuality are no mystery to Him; and one day they will no longer be a mystery to you. The mould in which a key is made would be a strange thing, if you had never seen a key: and the key itself a strange thing if you had never seen a lock. Your soul has a curious shape because it is a hollow made to fit a particular swelling in the infinite contours of the Divine substance, or a key to unlock one of the doors in the house with many mansions. For it is not humanity in the abstract that is to be saved, but you—you, the individual reader, John Stubbs or Janet Smith. Blessed and fortunate creature, your eyes shall behold Him and not another's. All that you are, sins apart, is destined, if you will let God have his good way, to utter satisfaction. The Brocken spectre "looked to every man like his first love", because she was a cheat. But God will look to every soul like its first love because He is its first love. Your place in heaven will seem to be made for you and you alone, because you were made for it—made for it stitch by stitch as a glove is made for a hand.

It is from this point of view that we can understand hell in its aspect of privation. All your life an unattainable ecstasy has hovered just beyond the grasp of your consciousness. The day is coming when you will wake to find, beyond all hope, that you have attained it, or else, that it was within your reach and you have lost it forever.

This may seem a perilously private and subjective notion of the pearl of great price, but it is not. The thing I am speaking of is not an experience. You have experienced only the *want* of it. The thing itself has never actually been embodied in any thought, or image, or emotion. Always it has summoned you out of yourself. And if you will not go out of yourself to follow it, if you sit down to brood on the desire and attempt to cherish it, the desire itself will evade you. "The door into life generally opens behind us" and "the only wisdom" for one "haunted with the scent of unseen roses, is work." This secret fire goes out when you use the bellows: bank it down with what seems unlikely fuel of dogma and ethics, turn your back on it and attend to your duties, and then it will blaze. The world is like a picture with a golden background, and we the figures in the picture. Until you step off the plane of the picture into the large dimensions of death you cannot see the gold. But we have reminders of it. To change our metaphor, the black-out is not quite complete. There are chinks. At times the daily scene looks big with its secret.

Such is my opinion; and it may be erroneous. Perhaps this secret desire also is part of the Old Man and must be crucified before the end. But this opinion has a curious trick of evading denial. The desire—much more the satisfaction—has always refused to be fully present in any experience. Whatever you try to identify with it, turns out to be not it but something else: so that hardly any degree of crucifixion or transformation could go beyond what the desire itself leads us to anticipate. Again, if this opinion is not true, something better is. But "something better"—not this or that experience, but beyond it—is almost the definition of the thing I am trying to describe.

The thing you long for summons you away from the self. Even the desire for the thing lives only if you abandon it. This is the ultimate law—the seed dies to live, the bread must be cast upon the waters, he that loses his soul will save it. But the life of the seed, the finding of the bread, the recovery of the soul, are as real as the preliminary sacrifice. Hence it is truly said of heaven "in heaven there is no ownership. If any there took upon him to call anything his own, he would straightway be thrust out into hell and become an evil spirit." But it is also said "To him that overcometh I will give a white stone, and in the stone a new name written, which no man knoweth saving he that receiveth it". What can be more a man's own than this new name which even in eternity remains a secret between God and him? And what shall we take this secrecy to mean? Surely, that each of the redeemed shall forever know and praise some one aspect of the Divine beauty better than any other creature can. Why else were individuals created, but that God, loving all infinitely, should love each differently? And this difference, so far from impairing, floods with meaning the love of all blessed creatures for one another, the communion of the saints. If all experienced God in the same way and returned Him an identical worship, the song of the Church triumphant would have no symphony, it would be like an orchestra in which all the instruments played the same note. Aristotle has told us that a city is a unity of unlikes, and St Paul that a body is a unity of different members. Heaven is a city, and a Body, because the blessed remain eternally different: a society, because each has something to tell all the others—fresh and ever fresh news of the "My God" whom each finds in Him who all praise as "Our God". For doubtless the continually successful, yet never complete, attempt by each soul to communicate its unique vision to all others (and that by means whereof earthly art and philosophy are but clumsy imitations) is also among the ends for which the individual was created.

For union exists only between distincts; and, perhaps, from this point of view, we catch a momentary glimpse of the meaning of all things. Pantheism is a creed not so much false as hopelessly behind the times. Once, before creation, it would have been true to say that everything was God. But God created: He caused things to be other than Himself that, being distinct, they might learn to love Him, and achieve union instead of mere sameness. Thus He also cast His bread upon the waters. Even within the creation we might say that inanimate matter, which has no will, is one with God in a sense in which men are not. But it is not God's purpose that we should go back into that old identity (as, perhaps, some Pagan mystics would have us do) but that we should go on to the maximum distinctness there to be reunited with Him in a higher

fashion. Even within the Holy One Himself, it is not sufficient that the Word should *be* God, it must also be *with*
God. The Father eternally begets the Son and the Holy
Ghost proceeds: deity introduces distinction within itself
so that the union of reciprocal loves may transcend mere
arithmetical unity or self-identity.

But the eternal distinctness of each soul—the secret
which makes of the union between each soul and God
a species in itself—will never abrogate the law that for-
bids ownership in heaven. As to its fellow-creatures, each
soul, we suppose, will be eternally engaged in giving away
to all the rest that which it receives. And as to God, we
must remember that the soul is but a hollow which God
fills. Its union with God is, almost by definition, a continual self-abandonment—an opening, an unveiling, a surrender, of itself. A blessed spirit is a mould ever more and
more patient of the bright metal poured into it, a body
ever more completely uncovered to the meridian blaze
of the spiritual sun. We need not suppose that the necessity for something analogous to self-conquest will ever be
ended, or that eternal life will not also be eternal dying. It
is in this sense that, as there may be pleasures in hell (God
shield us from them), there may be something not all unlike pains in heaven (God grant us soon to taste them).

For in self-giving, if anywhere, we touch a rhythm not
only of all creation but of all being. For the Eternal Word
also gives Himself in sacrifice; and that not only on Cal-
vary. For when He was crucified He "did that in the wild
weather of His outlying provinces which He had done
at home in glory and gladness". From before the foundation of the world He surrenders begotten Deity back

to begetting Deity in obedience. And as the Son glorifies the Father, so also the Father glorifies the Son. And, with submission, as becomes a layman, I think it was truly said "God loveth not Himself as Himself but as Goodness; and if there were aught better than God, He would love that and not Himself". From the highest to the lowest, self exists to be abdicated and, by that abdication, becomes the more truly self, to be thereupon yet the more abdicated, and so forever. This is not a heavenly law which we can escape by remaining earthly, nor an earthly law which we can escape by being saved. What is outside the system of self-giving is not earth, nor nature, nor "ordinary life", but simply and solely hell. Yet even hell derives from this law such reality as it has. That fierce imprisonment in the self is but the obverse of the self-giving which is absolute reality; the negative shape which the outer darkness takes by surrounding and defining the shape of the real, or which the real imposes on the darkness by having a shape and positive nature of its own.

The golden apple of selfhood, thrown among the false gods, became an apple of discord because they scrambled for it. They did not know the first rule of the holy game, which is that every player must by all means touch the ball and then immediately pass it on. To be found with it in your hands is a fault: to cling to it, death. But when it flies to and fro among the players too swift for eye to follow, and the great master Himself leads the revelry, giving Himself eternally to His creatures in the generation, and back to Himself in the sacrifice, of the Word, then indeed the eternal dance "makes heaven drowsy with the harmony". All pains and pleasures we have known on earth are early initiations in the movements of that dance: but the dance itself is strictly incomparable with the sufferings of this present time. As we draw nearer to its uncreated rhythm, pain and pleasure sink almost out of sight. There is joy in the dance, but it does not exist for the sake of joy. It does not even exist for the sake of good, or of love. It is Love Himself, and Good Himself, and therefore happy. It does not exist for us, but we for it. The size and emptiness of the universe which frightened us at the outset of this book, should awe us still, for though they may be no more than a subjective bye-product of our three-dimensional imagining, yet they symbolise great truth. As our Earth is to all the stars, so doubtless are we men and our concerns to all creation; as all the stars are to space itself, so are all creatures, all thrones and powers and mightiest of the created gods, to the abyss of the self-existing Being, who is to us Father and Redeemer and indwelling Comforter, but of whom no man nor angel can say nor conceive what He is in and for Himself, or what is the work that he "maketh from the beginning to the end". For they are all derived and unsubstantial things. Their vision fails them and they cover their eyes from the intolerable light of utter actuality, which was and is and shall be, which never could have been otherwise, which has no opposite.

IV

THE GOLDEN KEY

"If you love someone, you don't want them to suffer. You want to take their sufferings on yourself. If even I feel like that, why doesn't God?"

— *"Shadowlands"* (the movie)

"The Golden Key" to "The Land from Which the Shadows Fall"

THE REAL C. S. LEWIS never asked that question (on page 115), because he already knew the answer: that God *had* taken our sufferings on himself, on the Cross. The distinctive Christian answer to "the problem of pain" (Part V) is Christ. Christ is the tears of God.

Christ is also the answer to the question, "How do you *get* to this Heaven dimly sensed in Part I, longed for in Part II, and described in Part III? He is "the golden key". He himself asserted, "I am the Way", and "I am the Door." If this is true, Christianity is true, for this is the essence of Christianity. If this is not true, Christ is a liar or a lunatic.

"The Golden Key"

We begin with a fairy tale from the man Lewis always acknowledged as his spiritual master, George MacDonald. Even those who dislike MacDonald's Victorian style (like Tolkien) call this tale a masterpiece.

The key to the story is not in the story itself. It is that "the golden key" is Christ. However, instead of the usual Quest story, which begins with a question or problem (like how to open a door) and quests for its solution (the key), in this one the protagonists begin with the answer (the golden key) and quest for the question. This seems to imply that life is a quest for the door that Christ opens, a quest for Heaven. Christ has already been given to us, two thousand years ago; we now have to learn how to *use* this Heavenly key.

The introductory setting for the story, so healing and restorative for our cold times, was written by Lint Hatcher, editor of *Wonder* Magazine.

IT IS EARLY WINTER—about 3 weeks before Christmas—in the Year of Our Lord 1866. Outside the window, a light fragrant snow sifts softly down out of a dark, crisp Scottish sky. A patch of the blanketed garden outside is lit in a bright festive gold where the firelight from the parlour pours through onto it. You are in that parlour; warm, safe, filled, merry, and loved.

The smells of the now-consumed supper just finished (a

This introduction to George MacDonald's "The Golden Key" is by Lint Hatcher, *Wonder* magazine, Spring 1990, pp. 32–33.

lovely hot Shepherd's Pie) linger in the air, as the sounds of pans and plates come clattering out of the kitchen where Mother and the older girls are washing up. You can hear Mother singing quietly. Yours is a very large family (eleven children born to Mother in all, though two have already died in infancy) and your brothers are also working at various chores; Greville (the oldest) is outside getting more coal, "Sandy" is putting the horse to bed. Everyone is busy except you, the youngest. You sit, very happy and cozy, in front of the grate watching the crackling fire, anxiously anticipating the evening ahead, and simply musing on how good it is to have Scotland for your home, Victoria for your Queen, and George MacDonald for your father.

Father. For you the word still has the ancient meaning of saner, safer times. It sounds to you like the word "King". Your father loves you more than life itself, and you know it. You love him so, that you rush to him when he enters the room, cling to the wool leg of his trousers, beg to be held and allowed to bury your face in his long beard, the beard that visually connects him with pictures of Patriarchs in the family Bible; David, Moses, Solomon. You are not a sideline in his life, not what he does when he is not working; you are the reason he works. He plays with you, prays for you, he kisses you, he teaches you. He tells you where you came from, and why. He makes certain you will not die without ever knowing why you were born. He is sometimes grave, sometimes joking and jovial, sometimes sad, always wise, kind, and anxious to be with you. You will not know it for many years, but your father, George MacDonald—novelist, poet, theologian, myth-maker —will be called "the father of modern fantasy", will be called "master" by C. S. Lewis and will inspire and influence J. R. R. Tolkien, W. H. Auden, Lloyd Alexander. He will be called one of the greatest and noblest men of the nineteenth century. You will not know it,—but it would not surprise you. He is such a wonderful father.

The after-supper chores are concluding. The entire family is trickling gradually but purposefully into the parlour to help you sit by the fire. Greville comes in from the snow, shaking it off his shoulders and stamping it from his feet, and dumps more coal in the grate. Mother and the eldest girls take out knitting and needlepoint. Ian sits closest to the fire so that the shavings from his eternal whittling ("I declare, this lad is whittling-mad," father would say . . .) will fall onto the hearth. Father is the last into the room; he has taken a few moments to write—he is, though you are not aware of it—struggling to make ends meet for you all, always under the shadow of debt and ever-present publishers' deadlines that will make his novels seem like hack-work to some modern critics. But now, in the presence of his family, every shadow of care falls from his face. He sits in the largest chair—his chair—and takes you on his knee. You put your hand under his vest as you snuggle against him; you can feel his heart beating there.

"Is Uncle Dodgson coming tonight?" asks Mary.

"Yes, we want to hear more of his *Alice* story!"

Your father's friend Rev. Charles Dodgson, your sad-eyed but very funny "Uncle Dodgson" with the riotous imagination and always bearing gifts for children, will be known to the world someday as Lewis Carroll, and "the *Alice* story" is his handwritten manuscript of *Alice's Adventures Underground* which will soon be *Alice's Adventures in Wonderland.* You don't know it, but you have gotten a preview of one of the world's great books. You don't know it,—but it would not surprise you. Uncle Dodgson is a friend of Father's.

"No, my dears. He is still in Oxford. He will not be back for a fortnight, I fear," says Father.

Everyone groans. Two weeks seems an eternity when you

are a child—especially a child hearing *Alice in Wonderland*, as many of us ex-children will testify.

"Will we have other visitors tonight, Father?"

Visits from Father's friends are always special. Some of them, like Mr. Morris and the American Mr. Henry W. Longfellow, are almost as miraculous for children as are Uncle Dodgson's. Others, like those from Mr. Carlyle and Mr. Ralph Waldo Emerson, are quiet and mysterious to you youngsters; Father and grand poets talking in words which, while unintelligible to you, always seem full of bottomless significance.

"No, children. We are together alone tonight."

"Do you have a new story for us, Papa?"

Everyone falls silent. This is indeed a great hope.

"Why, you know, I do seem to have a new tale."

There is great exultation in the parlour. A new story from Father is a wonderful occasion at your house.

"It's been racing around in my head like a squirrel for a week now, distracting me from my work. It must come out—tonight!"

Loud hurrahs.

"What's it called, Papa?"

"Is it another story of Fairyland?"

"Are there ghosts or trolls?"

"Will it make us cry?"

"You must wait and see," Father says.

Everyone sits up alertly as Father rises and stands before the fireplace. There is a bright sparkle in his eyes. He is never happier than when telling you one of his stories.

You do not know it yet, but your Father will suffer much over the next 30 years before his death—his health will fail, he will never overcome his financial burdens, two more of you, his beloved children, will die. But he will remain astonishingly, extraordinarily happy, happy in a way that passes all understanding, happy in a way that will perhaps be impossible in the last half of the 20th Century. He will live as if the story he is about to tell is true . . . or as if something even better is.

"Someone get out some of those chestnuts," he demands. "We will roast them over the fire while I tell you the story of the golden key . . ."

———————

T HERE WAS A BOY who used to sit in the twilight and listen to his great-aunt's stories.

She told him that if he could reach the place where the end of the rainbow stands he would find there a golden key.

"And what is the key for?" the boy would ask. "What is it the key of? What will it open?"

"That nobody knows," his aunt would reply. "He has to find that out."

"I suppose, being gold," the boy once said, thoughtfully, "that I could get a good deal of money for it if I sold it."

"Better never find it than sell it," returned his aunt.

And the boy went to bed and dreamed about the golden key.

Now all that his great-aunt told the boy about the golden key would have been nonsense, had it not been that their little house stood on the borders of Fairyland. For it is perfectly well known that out of Fairyland nobody ever can find where the rainbow stands. The creature takes such

The Golden Key by George MacDonald, with pictures by Maurice Sendak, Afterword by W. H. Auden (New York: Farrar, Straus and Giroux, 1967).

good care of its golden key, always flitting from place to place, lest anyone should find it! But in Fairyland it is quite different. Things that look real in this country look very thin indeed in Fairyland, while some of the things that here cannot stand still for a moment, will not move there. So it was not in the least absurd of the old lady to tell her nephew such things about the golden key.

"Did you ever know any body to find it?" he asked, one evening.

"Yes. Your father, I believe, found it."

"And what did he do with it, can you tell me?"

"He never told me."

"What was it like?"

"He never showed it to me."

"How does a new key come there always?"

"I don't know. There it is."

"Perhaps it is the rainbow's egg."

"Perhaps it is. You will be a happy boy if you find the nest."

"Perhaps it comes tumbling down the rainbow from the sky."

"Perhaps it does."

One eveing, in the summer, he went into his own room and stood at the lattice-window, and gazed into the forest which fringed the outskirts of Fairyland. It came close up to his great-aunt's garden, and, indeed, sent some straggling trees into it. The forest lay to the east, and the sun, which was setting behind the cottage, looked straight into the dark wood with his level red eye. The trees were all old, and had few branches below, so that the sun could see a great way into the forest and the boy, being keen-sighted, could see almost as far as the sun. The trunks stood like rows of red columns in the shine of the red sun, and he could see down aisle after aisle in the vanishing distance. And as he gazed into the forest he began to feel as if the trees were all waiting for him, and had something they could not go on with til he came to them. But he was hungry and wanted his supper. So he lingered.

Suddenly, far among the trees, as far as the sun could shine, he saw a glorious thing. It was the end of a rainbow, large and brilliant. He could count all the seven colours, and could see shade after shade beyond the violet; while before the red stood a colour more gorgeous and mysterious still. It was a colour he had never seen before. Only the spring of the rainbow-arch was visible. He could see nothing of it above the trees.

"The golden key!" he said to himself, and darted out of the house and into the wood.

He had not gone far before the sun set. But the rainbow only glowed the brighter. For the rainbow of Fairyland is not dependent upon the sun, as ours is. The trees welcomed him. The bushes made way for him. The rainbow grew larger and brighter; and at length he found himself within two trees of it.

It was a grand sight, burning away there in silence, with its gorgeous, its lovely, its delicate colours, each distinct, all combining. He could now see a great deal more of it. It rose high into the blue heavens, but bent so little that he could not tell how high the crown of the arch must reach. It was still only a small portion of a huge bow.

He stood gazing at it till he forgot himself with delight —even forgot the key which he had come to seek. And as he stood it grew more wonderful still. For in each of the colours, which was as large as the column of a church, he could faintly see beautiful forms slowly ascending as if by the steps of a winding stair. The forms appeared irregularly—now one, now many, now several, now none—men and women and children—all different, all beautiful.

He drew nearer to the rainbow. It vanished. He started back a step in dismay. It was there again, as beautiful as ever. So he contented himself with standing as near it as he might, and watching the forms that ascended the glorious colours towards the unknown height of the arch, which did not end abruptly, but faded away in the blue air, so gradually that he could not say where it ceased.

When the thought of the golden key returned, the boy very wisely proceeded to mark out in his mind the space covered by the foundation of the rainbow, in order that he might know where to search, should the rainbow disappear. It was based chiefly upon a bed of moss.

Meantime it had grown quite dark in the wood. The rainbow alone was visible by its own light. But the moment the moon rose the rainbow vanished. Nor could any change of place restore the vision to the boy's eyes. So he threw himself down upon the mossy bed, to wait until the sunlight would give him a chance of finding the key. There he fell fast asleep.

When he woke in the morning the sun was looking straight into his eyes. He turned away from it, and the same moment saw a brilliant little thing lying on the moss within a foot of his face. It was the golden key. The pipe of it was of plain gold, as bright as gold could be. The handle was curiously wrought and set with sapphires. In a terror of delight he put out his hand and took it, and had it.

He lay for a while, turning it over and over, and feeding his eyes upon its beauty. Then he jumped to his feet, remembering that the pretty thing was of no use to him yet. Where was the lock to which the key belonged? It must be somewhere, for how could anybody be so silly as to make a key for which there was no lock? Where should he go to look for it? He gazed about him, up into the air, down to the earth, but saw no keyhole in the clouds, in the grass, or in the trees.

Just as he began to grow disconsolate, however, he saw something glimmering in the wood. It was a mere glimmer that he saw, but he took it for a glimmer of rainbow, and went towards it.—And now I will go back to the borders of the forest.

Not far from the house where the boy had lived, there was another house, the owner of which was a merchant, who was much away from home. He had lost his wife some years before, and had only one child, a little girl, whom he left to the charge of two servants, who were very idle and careless. So she was neglected and left untidy, and was sometimes ill-used besides.

Now it is well known that the little creatures commonly known as fairies, though there are many different kinds of fairies in Fairyland, have an exceeding dislike to untidiness. Indeed, they are quite spiteful to slovenly people. Being used to all the lovely ways of the trees and flowers, and to the neatness of the birds and all woodland creatures, it makes them feel miserable, even in their deep woods and on their grassy carpets, to think that within the same moonlight lies a dirty, uncomfortable, slovenly house. And this makes them angry with the people that live in it, and they would gladly drive them out of the world if they could. They want the whole earth nice and clean. So they pinch the maids black and blue and play them all manner of uncomfortable tricks.

But this house was quite a shame and the fairies of the forest could not endure it. They tried everything on the maids without effect, and at last resolved upon making a clean riddance, beginning with the child. They ought to have known that it was not her fault, but they have little principle and much mischief in them, and they thought that if they got rid of her the maids would be sure to be turned away.

So one evening, the poor little girl having been put to bed early, before the sun was down, the servants went off to the village, locking the door behind them. The child did not know she was alone, and lay contentedly looking out her window towards the forest, of which, however, she could not see much, because of the ivy and other creeping plants which had straggled across her window. All at once she saw an ape making faces at her out of the mirror, and the heads carved upon a great old wardrobe grinning fearfully. Then two old spider-legged chairs came forward into the middle of the room, and began to dance a queer, old-fashioned dance. This set her laughing and she forgot the ape and the grinning heads. So the fairies saw they had made a mistake, and sent the chairs back to their places. But they knew that she had been reading the story of Silverhair all day. So the next moment she heard the voices of the three bears upon the stair, big voice, middle voice, and little voice, and she heard their soft, heavy tread, as if they had stockings over their boots, coming nearer and nearer to the door of her room, till she could bear it no longer. She did just as Silverhair did, and the fairies wanted her to do; she darted to the window, pulled it open, got upon the ivy, and so scrambled to the ground. She then fled to the forest as fast as she could run.

Now, although she did not know it, this was the very best way she could have gone; for nothing is ever so mischievous in its own place as it is out of it; and, besides, these mischievous creatures were only the children of Fairyland, as it were, and there are many other beings there as well; and if a wanderer gets in among them, the good ones will always help him more than the evil ones will be able to hurt him.

The sun was now set, and the darkness coming on, but the child thought of no danger but the bears behind her. If she had looked round, however, she would have seen that she was followed by a very different creature from a bear. It was a curious creature, made like a fish, but covered, instead of scales, with feathers of all colours, sparkling like those of a humming-bird. It had fins, not wings, and swam through the air as a fish does through the water. Its head was like the head of a small owl.

After running a long way, and as the last of the light was disappearing, she passed under a tree with drooping branches. It dropped its branches to the ground all about her, and caught her as in a trap. She struggled to get out, but the branches pressed her closer and closer to the trunk. She was in great terror and distress, when the air-fish, swimming into the thicket of branches, began tearing them with its beak. They loosened their hold at once, and the creature went on attacking them, till at length they let the child go. Then the air-fish came from behind her, and swam on in front, glittering and sparkling all lovely colours; and she followed.

It led her gently along until all at once it swam in at a cottage-door. The child followed still. There was a bright fire in the middle of the floor, upon which stood a pot without a lid, full of water that boiled and bubbled furiously. The air-fish swam straight to the pot and into the boiling water, where it lay quiet. A beautiful woman rose from the opposite side of the fire and came to meet the girl. She took her up in her arms, and said,—

"Ah, you are come at last! I have been looking for you for a long time."

She sat down with her on her lap, and there the girl sat staring at her. She had never seen anything so beautiful. She was tall and strong, with white arms and neck, and a delicate flush on her face. The child could not tell what was the colour of her hair, but could not help thinking it had a tinge of dark green. She had not one ornament upon her, but she looked as if she had just put off quantities of diamonds and emeralds. Yet here she was in the simplest, poorest little cottage, where she was evidently at home. She was dressed in shining green.

The girl looked at the lady, and the lady looked at the girl.

"What is your name?" asked the lady.

"The servants always called me Tangle."

"Ah, that was because your hair was so untidy. But that was their fault, the naughty women! Still, it is a pretty

name, and I will call you Tangle too. You must not mind
my asking you questions, for you may ask me the same
questions, every one of them, and any others that you
like. How old are you?"

"Ten," answered Tangle.

"You don't look like it," said the lady.

"How old are you, please?" returned Tangle.

"Thousands of years old," answered the lady.

"You don't look like it," said Tangle.

"Don't I? I think I do. Don't you see how beautiful I
am?"

And her great blue eyes looked down on the little Tangle, as if all the stars in the sky were melted in them to
make their brightness.

"Ah! but," said Tangle, "when people live long, they
grow old. At least I always thought so."

"I have no time to grow old," said the lady. "I am too
busy for that. It is very idle to grow old.—but I cannot
have my little girl so untidy. Do you know I can't find a
clean spot on your face to kiss?"

"Perhaps," suggested Tangle, feeling ashamed, but not
too much so to say a word for herself—"perhaps that is
because the tree made me cry so."

"My poor darling!" said the lady, looking now as if the
moon were melted in her eyes, and kissing her little face,
dirty as it was, "the naughty tree must suffer for making
a girl cry."

"And what is your name please?" asked Tangle.

"Grandmother," answered the lady.

"Is it really?"

"Yes, indeed. I never tell stories, even in fun."

"How good of you!"

"I couldn't if I tried. It would come true if I said it, and then I should be punished enough."

And she smiled like the sun through a summer shower.

"But now," she went on "I must get you washed and dressed, and then we shall have some supper."

"Oh! I had supper long ago," said Tangle.

"Yes, indeed you had," answered the lady—"three years ago. You don't know that it is three years since you ran away from the bears. You are thirteen and more now."

Tangle could only stare. She felt quite sure it was true.

"You will not be afraid of anything I do with you—will you?" said the lady.

"I will try very hard not to be; but I can't be certain, you know," replied Tangle.

"I like your saying so, and I shall be quite satisfied," answered the lady.

She took off the girl's night-gown, rose with her in her arms, and going to the wall of the cottage, opened a door. Then Tangle saw a deep tank, the sides of which were filled with green plants, which had flowers of all colours. There was a roof over it like the roof of the cottage. It was filled with beautiful clear water, in which swam a multitude of such fishes as the one that had led her to the cottage. It was the light their colours gave that showed the place in which they were.

The lady spoke some words Tangle could not understand, and threw her into the tank.

The fishes came crowding about her. Two or three of them got under her head and kept it up. The rest of them rubbed themselves all over her, and with their wet feathers washed her quite clean. Then the lady, who had been looking on all the time, spoke again; whereupon some thirty or forty of the fishes rose out of the water underneath Tangle, and so bore her up to the arms the lady held out to take her. She carried her back to the fire, and, having dried her well, opened a chest, and taking out the finest linen garments, smelling of grass and lavender, put them upon her, and over all a green dress, just like her own, shining like hers, and soft like hers, and going into such lovely folds from the waist, where it was tied with a brown cord, to her bare feet.

"Won't you give me a pair of shoes too, Grandmother?" said Tangle.

"No, my dear; no shoes. Look here. I wear no shoes."

So saying, she lifted her dress a little, and there were the loveliest white feet, but no shoes. Then Tangle was content to go without shoes too. And the lady sat down with her again, and combed her hair, and brushed it, and then left it to dry while she got the supper.

First she got bread out of one hole in the wall; then milk out of another; then several kinds of fruit out of a third; and then she went to the pot on the fire, and took out the fish now nicely cooked, and, as soon as she had pulled off its feathered skin, ready to be eaten.

"But," exclaimed Tangle. And she stared at the fish but could say no more.

"I know what you mean," returned the lady. "You do not like to eat the messenger that brought you home. But it is the kindest return you can make. The creature was afraid to go until it saw me put the pot on, and heard me promise it should be boiled the moment it returned with

you. Then it darted out of the door at once. You saw it
go into the pot of itself the moment it entered, did you
not?"

"I did," answered Tangle, "and I thought it very strange;
but then I saw you, and forgot all about the fish."

"In Fairyland," resumed the lady, as they sat down to
the table, "the ambition of the animals is to be eaten by the
people; for that is their highest end in that condition. But
they are not therefore destroyed. Out of that pot comes
something more than the dead fish, you will see."

Tangle now remarked that the lid was on the pot. But
the lady took no further notice of it till they had eaten the
fish, which Tangle found nicer than any fish she had ever
tasted before. It was as white as snow, and as delicate as
cream. And the moment she had swallowed a mouthful
of it, a change she could not describe began to take place
in her. She heard a murmuring all about her, which became more and more articulate, and at length, as she went
on eating, grew intelligible. By the time she had finished
her share, the sounds of all the animals in the forest came
crowding through the door to her ears; for the door still
stood wide open, though it was pitch-dark outside; and
they were no longer sounds only; they were speech, and
speech that she could understand. She could tell what the
insects in the cottage were saying to each other too. She
had even a suspicion that the trees and flowers all about
the cottage were holding midnight communications with
each other; but what they said she could not hear.

As soon as the fish was eaten, the lady went to the fire
and took the lid off the pot. A lovely little creature in human shape, with large white wings, rose out of it, and flew

round and round the roof of the cottage; then dropped, fluttering, and nestled in the lap of the lady. She spoke to it some strange words, carried it to the door, and threw it out into the darkness. Tangle heard the flapping of its wings die away in the distance.

"Now have we done the fish any harm?" she said, returning.

"No," answered Tangle, "I do not think we have. I should not mind eating one every day."

"They must wait their time, like you and me too, my little Tangle."

And she smiled a smile which the sadness in it made more lovely.

"But," she continued, "I think we may have one for supper tomorrow."

So saying she went to the door of the tank, and spoke; and now Tangle understood her perfectly.

"I want one of you," she said,—"the wisest."

Thereupon the fishes got together in the middle of the tank, with their heads forming a circle above the water, and their tails a larger circle beneath it. They were holding a council, in which their relative wisdom should be determined. At length one of them flew up into the lady's hand, looking lively and ready.

"You know where the rainbow stands?" she asked.

"Yes, Mother, quite well," answered the fish.

"Bring home a young man you will find there, who does not know where to go."

The fish was out of the door in a moment. Then the lady told Tangle it was time to go to bed; and, opening another door in the side of the cottage, showed her a little

arbour, cool and green, with a bed of purple heath growing in it, upon which she threw a large wrapper made of
the feathered skins of the wise fishes, shining gorgeous in
the firelight. Tangle was soon lost in the strangest, loveliest dreams. And the beautiful lady was in every one of her
dreams.

In the morning she woke to the rustling of leaves over
her head, and the sound of running water. But, to her
surprise, she could find no door—nothing but the moss
grown wall of the cottage. So she crept through an opening in the arbour, and stood in the forest. Then she bathed
in a stream that ran merrily through the trees, and felt happier; for having once been in her grandmother's pond, she
must be clean and tidy ever after; and, having put on her
green dress, felt like a lady.

She spent that day in the wood, listening to the birds and
beasts and creeping things. She understood all that they
said, though she could not repeat a word of it; and every
kind had a different language, while there was a common
though more limited understanding between all the in-
habitants of the forest. She saw nothing of the beautiful
lady, but she felt that she was near her all the time; and
she took care not to go out of sight of the cottage. It was
round, like a snow-hut or a wigwam; and she could see
neither door nor window in it. The fact was, it had no
windows; and though it was full of doors, they all opened
from the inside, and could not even be seen from the outside.

She was standing at the foot of a tree in the twilight, listening to a quarrel between a mole and a squirrel, in which
the mole told the squirrel that the tail was the best of him,

and the squirrel called the mole Spade-fists, when, the darkness having deepened around her, she became aware of something shining in her face, and looking round, saw that the door of the cottage was open, and the red light of the fire flowing from it like a river through the darkness. She left Mole and Squirrel to settle matters as they might, and darted off to the cottage. Entering, she found the pot boiling on the fire, and the grand, lovely lady sitting on the other side of it.

"I've been watching you all day," said the lady. "You shall have something to eat by-and-by, but we must wait til our supper comes home."

She took Tangle on her knee, and began to sing to her— such songs as made her wish she could listen to them for ever. But at length in rushed the shining fish, and snuggled down in the pot. It was followed by a youth who had outgrown his worn garments. His face was ruddy with health, and in his hand he carried a little jewel, which sparkled in the firelight.

The first words the lady said were,—

"What is that in your hand, Mossy?"

Now Mossy was the name that his companions had given him, because he had a favourite stone covered with moss, on which he used to sit whole days reading; and they said the moss had begun to grow upon him too.

Mossy held out his hand. The moment the lady saw that it was the golden key, she rose from her chair, kissed Mossy on the forehead, made him sit down on her seat, and stood before him like a servant. Mossy could not bear this, and rose at once. But the lady begged him, with tears in her beautiful eyes, to sit, and let her wait on him.

"But you are a great, splendid, beautiful lady," said Mossy.

"Yes, I am. But I work all day long—that is my pleasure; and you will have to leave me so soon!"

"How do you know that, if you please, madam?" asked Mossy.

"Because you have got the golden key."

"But I don't know what it is for. I can't find the keyhole. Will you tell me what to do?"

"You must look for the keyhole. That is your work. I cannot help you. I can only tell you that if you look for it you will find it."

"What kind of a box will it open? What is there inside?"

"I do not know. I dream about it, but I know nothing."

"Must I go at once?"

"You may stop here tonight, and have some of my supper. But you must go in the morning. All I can do for you is to give you clothes. Here is a girl called Tangle, whom you must take with you."

"That *will* be nice," said Mossy.

"No, no!" said Tangle. "I don't want to leave you, please, Grandmother."

"You must go with him, Tangle. I am sorry to lose you, but it will be the best thing for you. Even the fishes, you see, have to go into the pot, and then out into the dark. If you fall in with the Old Man of the Sea, mind you ask him whether he has not got some more fishes ready for me. My tank is getting thin."

So saying, she took the fish from the pot, and put the lid on as before. They sat down and ate the fish, and then the winged creature rose from the pot, circled the roof, and settled on the lady's lap. She talked to it, carried it to the door, and threw it out into the dark. They heard the flap of its wings die away in the distance.

The lady then showed Mossy into just such another chamber as that of Tangle; and in the morning he found a suit of clothes laid beside him. He looked very handsome in them. But the wearer of Grandmother's clothes never thinks about how he or she looks, but thinks always how handsome other people are.

Tangle was very unwilling to go.

"Why should I leave you? I don't know the young man," she said to the lady.

"I am never allowed to keep my children long. You need not go with him except you please, but you must go some day; and I should like you to go with him, for he has found the golden key. No girl need be afraid to go with a youth that has the golden key. You will take care of her, Mossy, will you not?"

"That I will," said Mossy.

And Tangle cast a glance at him, and thought she should like to go with him.

"And," said the lady, "if you should lose each other as you go through the—the—I never can remember the name of that country,—do not be afraid, but go on and on."

She kissed Tangle on the mouth and Mossy on the forehead, led them to the door, and waved her hand eastward. Mossy and Tangle took each other's hand and walked away into the depth of the forest. In his right hand Mossy held the golden key.

They wandered thus a long way, with endless amusement from the talk of the animals. They soon learned enough of their language to ask them necessary questions. The squirrels were always friendly, and gave them nuts out of their own hoards; but the bees were selfish and rude, justifying themselves on the ground that Tangle and Mossy were not subjects of their queen, and charity must begin at home, though indeed they had not one drone in their poorhouse at the time. Even the blinking moles would fetch them an earth-nut or a truffle now and then, talking as if their mouths, as well as their eyes and ears, were full of cotton wool, or their own velvety fur. By the time they got out of the forest they were very fond of each other, and Tangle was not in the least sorry that her grandmother had sent her away with Mossy.

At length the trees grew smaller, and stood farther apart, and the ground began to rise, and it got more and more steep, till the trees were all left behind, and the two were climbing a narrow path with rocks on each side. Suddenly they came upon a rude doorway, by which they entered a narrow gallery cut in the rock. It grew darker and darker, till it was pitch-dark, and they had to feel their way. At length the light began to return, and at last they came upon a narrow path on the face of a lofty precipice. This path went winding down the rock to a wide plain, circular in shape, and surrounded on all sides by mountains. Those opposite to them were a great way off, and towered to an awful height, shooting up sharp, blue, ice-enamelled pinnacles. An utter silence reigned where they stood. Not even the sound of water reached them.

Looking down, they could not tell whether the valley below was a grassy plain or a great still lake. They had

never seen any space look like it. The way to it was difficult and dangerous, but down the narrow path they went,
and reached the bottom in safety. They found it com-
posed of smooth, light-coloured sandstone, undulating in
parts, but mostly level. It was no wonder to them now
that they had not been able to tell what it was, for this
surface was everywhere crowded with shadows. It was a
sea of shadows. The mass was chiefly made up of the shadows of leaves innumerable, of all lovely and imaginative
forms, waving to and fro, floating and quivering in the
breath of a breeze whose motion was unfelt, whose sound
was unheard. No forests clothed the mountain-sides, no
trees were anywhere to be seen, and yet the shadows of
the leaves, branches, and stems of all various trees covered
the valley as far as their eyes could reach. They soon spied
the shadows of flowers mingled with those of the leaves,
and now and then the shadow of a bird with open beak,
and throat distended in song. At times would appear the
forms of strange, graceful creatures, running up and down
the shadow-boles and along the branches, to disappear in
the wind-tossed foliage. As they walked they waded knee-
deep in the lovely lake. For the shadows were not merely
lying on the surface of the ground, but heaped up above
it like substantial forms of darkness, as if they had been
cast upon a thousand different planes of air. Tangle and
Mossy often lifted their heads and gazed upwards to de-
scry whence the shadows came; but they could see nothing more than a bright mist spread above them, higher
than the tops of the mountains, which stood clear against
it. No forests, no leaves, no birds were visible.

After a while, they reached more open spaces, where

the shadows were thinner; and came even to portions over which shadows only flitted, leaving them clear for such as might follow. Now a wonderful form, half bird-like, half human, would float across on outspread sailing pinions. Anon an exquisite shadow group of gambolling children would be followed by the loveliest female form, and that again by the grand stride of a Titanic shape, each disappearing in the surrounding press of shadowy foliage. Sometimes a profile of unspeakable beauty or grandeur would appear for a moment and vanish. Sometimes they seemed lovers that passed linked arm in arm, sometimes father and son, sometimes brothers in loving contest, sometimes sisters entwined in gracefullest community of complex form. Sometimes wild horses would tear across, free, or bestrode by noble shadows of ruling men. But some of the things which pleased them most they never knew how to describe.

About the middle of the plain they sat down to rest in the heart of a heap of shadows. After sitting for a while, each, looking up, saw the other in tears; they were each longing after the country whence the shadows fell.

"We *must* find the country from which the shadows come," said Mossy.

"We must, dear Mossy," responded Tangle. "What if your golden key should be the key to *it*?"

"Ah, that would be grand," returned Mossy.

—"But we must rest here for a little, and then we shall be able to cross the plain before night."

So he lay down on the ground, and about him on every side, and over his head, was the constant play of the wonderful shadows. He could look through them, and see the one behind the other, till they mixed in a mass of darkness. Tangle, too, lay admiring, and wondering, and longing after the country whence the shadows came. When they were rested they rose and pursued their journey.

How long they were in crossing this plain I cannot tell; but before night Mossy's hair was streaked with gray and Tangle had got wrinkles on her forehead.

As evening drew on, the shadows fell deeper and rose higher. At length they reached a place where they rose above their heads, and made all dark around them. Then they took hold of each other's hand, and walked on in silence and in some dismay. They felt the gathering darkness, and something strangely solemn besides, and the beauty of the shadows ceased to delight them. All at once Tangle found that she had not a hold of Mossy's hand, though when she lost it she could not tell.

"Mossy, Mossy!" she cried aloud in terror.

But no Mossy replied.

A moment after, the shadows sank to her feet, and down under her feet, and the mountains rose before her. She turned towards the gloomy region she had left, and called once more upon Mossy. There the gloom lay tossing and heaving, a dark, stormy, foamless sea of shadows, but no Mossy rose out of it, or came climbing up the hill on which she stood. She threw herself down and wept in despair.

Suddenly she remembered that the beautiful lady had told them, if they lost each other in a country of which she could not remember the name, they were not to be afraid, but to go straight on.

"And besides," she said to herself, "Mossy has the

golden key, and so no harm will come to him, I do believe."

She rose from the ground, and went on.

Before long she arrived at a precipice, in the face of which a stair was cut. When she had ascended half-way, the stair ceased, and the path led straight into the mountain. She was afraid to enter, and turning again towards the stair, grew giddy at the sight of the depth beneath her, and was forced to throw herself down in the mouth of the cave.

When she opened her eyes, she saw a beautiful little creature with wings standing beside her, waiting.

"I know you," said Tangle. "You are my fish."

"Yes. But I am a fish no longer. I am an aëranth now."

"What is that?" asked Tangle.

"What you see I am," answered the shape. "And I am come to lead you through the mountain."

"Oh! thank you, dear fish—aëranth, I mean," returned Tangle, rising.

Thereupon the aëranth took to his wings, and flew on through the long narrow passage, reminding Tangle very much of the way he had swum on before when he was a fish. And the moment his white wings moved, they began to throw off a continuous shower of sparks of all colours, which lighted up the passage before them.—All at once he vanished, and Tangle heard a low sweet sound, quite different from the rush and crackle of his wings. Before her was an open arch, and through it came light, mixed with the sound of sea-waves.

She hurried out, and fell, tired and happy, upon the yellow sand of the shore. There she lay, half asleep with weariness and rest, listening to the low plash and retreat of the tiny waves, which seemed ever enticing the land to leave off being land, and become sea. And as she lay, her eyes were fixed upon the foot of a great rainbow standing far away against the sky on the other side of the sea. At length she fell fast asleep.

When she awoke, she saw an old man with long white hair down to his shoulders, leaning upon a stick covered with green buds, and so bending over her.

"What do you want here, beautiful woman?" he said.

"Am I beautiful? I am so glad!" answered Tangle, rising. "My grandmother is beautiful."

"Yes. But what do you want?" he repeated, kindly.

"I think I want you. Are you not the Old Man of the Sea?"

"I am."

"Then Grandmother says, have you any more fishes ready for her?"

"We will go and see, my dear," answered the Old Man, speaking yet more kindly than before. "And I can do something for you, can I not?"

"Yes—show me the way up to the country from which the shadows fall," said Tangle.

For there she hoped to find Mossy again.

"Ah! indeed, that would be worth doing," said the Old Man. "But I cannot, for I do not know the way myself. But I will send you to the Old Man of the Earth. Perhaps he can tell you. He is much older than I am."

Leaning on his staff, he conducted her along the shore to a steep rock, that looked like a petrified ship turned upside down. The door of it was the rudder of a great vessel, ages ago, at the bottom of the sea. Immediately within the door was a stair in the rock, down which the Old Man went, and Tangle followed. At the bottom the Old Man had his house, and there he lived.

As soon as she entered it, Tangle heard a strange noise, unlike anything she had ever heard before. She soon found that it was the fishes talking. She tried to understand what they said; but their speech was so old-fashioned, and rude, and undefined, that she could not make much of it.

"I will go and see about those fishes for my daughter," said the Old Man of the Sea.

And moving a slide in the wall of his house, he first looked out, and then tapped upon a thick piece of crystal that filled the round opening. Tangle came up behind him, and peeping through the window into the heart of the great deep green ocean, saw the most curious creatures, some very ugly, all very odd, and with especially queer mouths, swimming about everywhere, above and below, but all coming towards the window in answer to the tap of the Old Man of the Sea. Only a few could get their mouths against the glass; but those who were floating miles away yet turned their heads toward it. The Old Man looked through the whole flock carefully for some minutes, then turning to Tangle, said,—

"I am sorry I have not got one ready yet. I want more time than she does. But I will send some as soon as I can."

He then shut the slide.

Presently a great noise arose in the sea. The Old Man opened the slide again, and tapped on the glass, whereupon the fishes were all as still as sleep.

"They were only talking about you," he said. "And they

do speak such nonsense!—Tomorrow," he continued, "I must show you the way to the Old Man of the Earth. He lives a long way from here."

"Do let me go at once," said Tangle.

"No. That is not possible. You must come this way first."

He led her to a hole in the wall, which she had not observed before. It was covered with the green leaves and white blossoms of a creeping plant.

"Only white-blossoming plants can grow under the sea," said the Old Man. "In there you will find a bath, in which you must lie till I call you."

Tangle went in, and found a smaller room or cave, in the further corner of which was a great basin hollowed out of a rock, and half-full of the clearest sea-water. Little streams were constantly running into it from cracks in the wall of the cavern. It was polished quite smooth inside, and had a carpet of yellow sand in the bottom of it. Large green leaves and white flowers of various plants crowded up over it, draping and covering it almost entirely.

No sooner was she undressed and lying in the bath, than she began to feel as if the water were sinking into her, and she were receiving all the good of sleep without undergoing its forgetfulness. She felt the good coming all the time. And she grew happier and more hopeful than she had been since she lost Mossy. But she could not help thinking how very sad it was for a poor old man to live there all alone, and to have to take care of a whole seaful of stupid and riotous fishes.

After about an hour, as she thought, she heard his voice calling her, and rose out of the bath. All the fatigue and aching of her long journey had vanished. She was as whole, and strong, and well as if she had slept for seven days.

Returning to the opening that led into the other part of the house, she started back with amazement, for through it she saw the form of a grand man, with a majestic and beautiful face, waiting for her.

"Come," he said. "I see you are ready."

She entered with reverence.

"Where is the Old Man of the Sea?" she asked, humbly.

"There is no one here but me," he answered, smiling. "Some people call me the Old Man of the Sea. Others have another name for me and are terribly frightened when they meet me taking a walk by the shore. Therefore I avoid being seen by them, for they are so afraid, that they never see what I really am. You see me now.—But I must show you the way to the Old Man of the Earth."

He led her into the cave where the bath was, and there she saw, in the opposite corner, a second opening in the rock.

"Go down that stair, and it will bring you to him," said the Old Man of the Sea.

With humble thanks Tangle took her leave. She went down the winding stair, till she began to fear there was no end to it. Still down and down it went, rough and broken, with springs of water bursting out of the rocks and running down the steps beside her. It was quite dark about her, and yet she could see. For after being in that bath, people's eyes always give out a light they can see by. There were no creeping things in the way. All was safe and pleasant, though so dark and damp and deep.

At last there was not one step more, and she found herself in a glimmering cave. On a stone in the middle of it sat a figure with its back toward her—the figure of an old man bent double with age. From behind she could see his white beard spread out on the rocky floor in front of him. He did not move as she entered, so she passed round that she might stand before him and speak to him. The moment she looked in his face, she saw that he was a youth of marvellous beauty. He sat entranced with the delight of what he beheld in a mirror of something like silver, which lay on the floor at his feet, and which from behind she had taken for his white beard. He sat on, heedless of her presence, pale with the joy of his vision. She stood and watched him. At length, all trembling, she spoke. But her voice made no sound. Yet the youth lifted up his head. He showed no surprise, however, at seeing her—only smiled a welcome.

"Are you the Old Man of the Earth?" Tangle had said.

And the youth answered, and Tangle heard him, though not with her ears:—

"I am. What can I do for you?"

"Tell me the way to the country whence the shadows fall."

"Ah! That I do not know. I only dream about it myself. I see its shadows sometimes in my mirror: the way to it I do not know. But I think the Old Man of the Fire must know. He is much older than I am. He is the oldest man of all."

"Where does he live?"

"I will show you the way to his place. I never saw him myself."

So saying, the young man rose, and then stood for a while gazing at Tangle.

"I wish I could see that country too," he said. "But I must mind my work."

He led her to the side of the cave, and told her to lay her ear against the wall.

"What do you hear?" he asked.

"I hear," answered Tangle, "the sound of a great water running inside the rock."

"That river runs down to the dwelling of the oldest man of all—the Old Man of the Fire. I wish I could go to see him. But I must mind my work. That river is the only way to him."

Then the Old Man of the Earth stooped over the floor of the cave, raised a huge stone from it, and left it leaning. It disclosed a great hole that went plumb-down.

"That is the way," he said.

"But there are no stairs."

"You must throw yourself in. There is no other way."

She turned and looked him full in the face—stood so for a whole minute, as she thought: it was a whole year —then threw herself headlong into the hole.

When she came to herself, she found herself gliding down fast and deep. Her head was underwater, but that did not signify, for, when she thought about it she could not remember that she had breathed once since her bath in the cave of the Old Man of the Sea. When she lifted up her head a sudden and fierce heat struck her, and she sank it again instantly, and went sweeping on.

Gradually the stream grew shallower. At length she could hardly keep her head under. Then the water could carry her no farther. She rose from the channel and went step for step down the burning descent. The water ceased altogether. The heat was terrible. She felt scorched to the bone, but it did not touch her strength. It grew hotter and hotter. She said "I can bear it no longer." Yet she went on.

At the long last, the stair ended at a rude archway in an all but glowing rock. Through this archway Tangle fell exhausted into a cool mossy cave. The floor and walls were covered with moss—green, soft, and damp. A little stream spouted from a rent in the rock and fell into a basin of moss. She plunged her face into it and drank. Then she lifted her head and looked around. Then she rose and looked again. She saw no one in the cave. But the moment she stood upright she had a marvellous sense that she was in the secret of the earth and all its ways. Everything that she had seen, or learned from books; all that her grandmother had said or sung to her; all the talk of the beasts, birds, and fishes; all that had happened to her on her journey with Mossy, and since then in the heart of the earth with the old man and the older man—all was plain: she understood it all, and saw that everything meant the same thing, though she could not have put it into words again.

The next moment she descried, in a corner of the cave, a little naked child, sitting on the moss. He was playing with balls of various colours and sizes, which he disposed in strange figures on the floor beside him. And now Tangle felt that there was something in her knowledge which was not in her understanding. For she knew there must be an infinite meaning in the change and sequence and individual forms of the figures into which the child arranged the balls, as well as in the varied harmonies of their colours, but what it all meant she could not tell.[1] He went on busily, tirelessly, playing his solitary game, without looking up, or seeming to know that there was a stranger in his deep-withdrawn cell. Diligently as a lace-maker shifts her bobbins, he shifted and arranged his balls. Flashes of meaning would now pass from them to Tangle, and now again all would be not merely obscure, but utterly dark. She stood looking for a long time, for there was fascination in the sight; and the longer she looked the more an indescribable vague intelligence went on rousing itself in her mind. For seven years she had stood there watching the naked child with his coloured balls, and it seemed to her like seven hours, when all at once the shape the balls took, she knew not why, reminded her of the Valley of Shadows, and she spoke:—

"Where is the Old Man of the Fire?" she said.

"Here I am," answered the child, rising and leaving the balls on the moss. "What can I do for you?"

There was such an awfulness of absolute repose on the face of the child that Tangle stood dumb before him. He had no smile, but the love in his large gray eyes was deep as the center. And with the repose there lay on his face a shimmer as of moonlight, which seemed as if any moment it might break into such a ravishing smile as would cause the beholder to weep himself to death. But the smile never came, and the moonlight lay there unbroken. For the heart of the child was too deep for any smile to reach from it to his face.

[1] I think I must be indebted to Novalis for these geometrical figures —G. MacDonald.

"Are you the oldest man of all?" Tangle at length, although filled with awe, ventured to ask.

"Yes, I am. I am very, very old. I am able to help you, I know. I can help everybody."

And the child drew near and looked up in her face so that she burst into tears.

"Can you tell me the way to the country the shadows fall from?" she sobbed.

"Yes. I know the way quite well. I go there myself sometimes. But you could not go my way; you are not old enough. I will show you how you can go."

"Do not send me out into the great heat again," prayed Tangle.

"I will not," answered the child.

And he reached up, and put his cool hand on her heart.

"Now," he said, "you can go. The fire will not burn you. Come."

He led her from the cave, and following him through another archway, she found herself in a vast desert of sand and rock. The sky of it was rock, lowering over them like solid thunderclouds; and the whole place was so hot that she saw, in bright rivulets, the yellow gold and white silver and red copper trickling molten from the rocks. But the heat never came near her.

When they had gone some distance, the child turned up a great stone, and took something like an egg from under it. He next drew a long curved line in the sand with his finger, and laid the egg in it. He then spoke something Tangle could not understand. The egg broke, a small snake came out, and, lying in the line in the sand, grew and grew till he filled it. The moment he was thus full-grown, he began to glide away, undulating like a sea-wave.

"Follow that serpent," said the child. "He will lead you the right way."

Tangle followed the serpent. But she could not go far without looking back at the marvellous child. He stood alone in the midst of the glowing desert, beside a fountain of red flame that had burst forth at his feet, his naked whiteness glimmering a pale rosy red in the torrid fire. There he stood, looking after her, till, from the lengthening distance, she could see him no more. The serpent went straight on, turning neither to the right nor left.

Meantime Mossy had got out of the lake of shadows and, following his mournful, lonely way, had reached the seashore. It was a dark, stormy evening. The sun had set. The wind was blowing from the sea. The waves had surrounded the rock within which lay the Old Man's house. A deep water rolled between it and the shore, upon which a majestic figure was walking alone.

Mossy went up to him and said,—

"Will you tell me where to find the Old Man of the Sea?"

"I am the Old Man of the Sea," the figure answered.

"I see a strong kingly man of middle age," returned Mossy.

Then the Old Man looked at him more intently, and said,—

"Your sight, young man, is better than that of most who take this way. The night is stormy: come to my house and tell me what I can do for you."

Mossy followed him. The waves flew from before the footsteps of the Old Man of the Sea, and Mossy followed upon dry sand.

When they had reached the cave, they sat down and gazed at each other.

Now Mossy was an old man by this time. He looked much older than the Old Man of the Sea, and his feet were very weary.

After looking at him for a moment, the Old Man took him by the hand and led him into his inner cave. There he helped him to undress, and laid him in the bath. And he saw that one of his hands Mossy did not open.

"What have you got in that hand?" he asked.

Mossy opened his hand, and there lay the golden key.

"Ah!" said the Old Man, "that accounts for your knowing me. And I know the way you have to go."

"I want to find the country whence the shadows fall," said Mossy.

"I daresay you do. So do I. But meantime, one thing is certain.—what is that key for, do you think?"

"For a keyhole somewhere. But I don't know why I keep it. I never could find the keyhole. And I have lived a good while, I believe," said Mossy sadly. "I'm not sure that I'm not old. I know my feet ache."

"Do they?" said the Old Man, as if he really meant to ask a question; and Mossy, who was still lying in the bath, watched his feet for a moment before he replied.

"No, they do not," he answered. "Perhaps I am not old either."

"Get up and look at yourself in the water."

He rose and looked at himself in the water, and there was not a gray hair on his head or a wrinkle on his skin.

"You have tasted of death now," said the Old Man. "Is it good?"

"It is good," said Mossy. "It is better than life."

"No," said the Old Man; "it is only more life.—Your feet will make no holes in the water now."

"What do you mean?"

"I will show you that presently."

They returned to the outer cave, and sat and talked together for a long time. At length the Old Man of the Sea arose, and said to Mossy,—

"Follow me."

He led him up the stair again, and opened another door. They stood on the level of the raging sea, looking towards the east. Across the waste of waters, against the bosom of a fierce black cloud, stood the foot of a rainbow, glowing in the dark.

"This indeed is my way," said Mossy, as soon as he saw the rainbow, and stepped out upon the sea. His feet made no holes in the water. He fought the wind, and clomb the waves, and went on towards the rainbow.

The storm died away. A lovely day and a lovelier night followed. A cool wind blew over the wide plain of the quiet ocean. And still Mossy journeyed eastward. But the rainbow had vanished with the storm.

Day after day he held on, and he thought he had no

guide. He did not see how a shining fish under the waters directed his steps. He crossed the sea, and came to a great precipice of rock, up which he could discover but one path. Nor did this lead him farther than half-way up the rock, where it ended on a platform. Here he stood and pondered.—It could not be that the way stopped here, else what was the path for? It was a rough path, not very plain, yet certainly a path.—He examined the face of the rock. It was smooth as glass. But as his eyes kept roving hopelessly over it, something glittered, and he caught sight of a row of small sapphires. They bordered a little hole in the rock.

"The keyhole!" he cried.

He tried the key. It fitted. It turned. A great clang and clash, as of iron bolts on huge brazen caldrons, echoed thunderously within. He drew out the key. The rock in front of him began to fall. He retreated from it as far as the breadth of the platform would allow. A great slab fell at his feet. In front was still the solid rock, with this one slab fallen forward out of it. But the moment he stepped upon it, a second fell, just short of the edge of the first, making the next step of a stair, which thus kept dropping itself before him as he ascended into the heart of the precipice. It led him into a hall fit for such an approach—irregular and rude in formation, but floor, sides, pillars, and vaulted roof, all one mass of shining stones of every colour that light can show. In the centre stood seven columns, ranged from red to violet. And on the pedestal of one of them sat a woman, motionless, with her face bowed upon her knees. Seven years she had sat there waiting. She lifted her head as Mossy drew near. It was Tangle. Her hair had grown to her feet, and was rippled like the windless sea on broad sands. Her face was beautiful, like her grand-mother's, and as still and peaceful as that of the Old Man of the Fire. Her form was tall and noble. Yet Mossy knew her at once.

"How beautiful you are Tangle!" he said, in delight and astonishment.

"Am I?" she returned. "Oh, I have waited for you for so long! But you, you are like the Old Man of the Sea. No. You are like the Old Man of the Earth. No, no. You are like the oldest man of all. You are like them all. And yet you are my own old Mossy! How did you come here? What did you do after I lost you? Did you find the key-hole? Have you got the key still?"

She had a hundred questions to ask him, and he a hun-dred more to ask her. They told each other all their ad-ventures, and were as happy as a man and woman could be. For they were younger and better, and stronger and wiser, than they had ever been before.

It began to grow dark. And they wanted more than ever to reach the country whence the shadows fall. So they looked about them for a way out of the cave. The door by which Mossy had entered had closed again, and there was a half a mile of rock between them and the sea. Nei-ther could Tangle find the opening in the floor by which the serpent had led her thither. They searched till it grew so dark that they could see nothing, and gave it up.

After a while, however, the cave began to glimmer again. The light came from the moon, but it did not look like moonlight, for it gleamed through those seven pillars in the middle, and filled the place with all colours. And now Mossy saw that there was a pillar beside the red one, which he had not observed before. And it was of the same new colour that he had seen in the rainbow when he saw it first in the fairy forest. And on it he saw a sparkle of blue. It was the sapphires round the keyhole.

He took his key. It turned in the lock to the sounds of Æolian music. A door opened upon slow hinges, and disclosed a winding stair within. The key vanished from his fingers. Tangle went up. Mossy followed. The door closed behind them. They climbed out of the earth; and still climbing, rose above it. They were in the rainbow. Far abroad, over ocean and land, they could see through its transparent walls the earth beneath their feet. Stairs beside stairs wound up together, and beautiful beings of all ages climbed along with them.

They knew that they were going up to the country whence the shadows fall.

And by this time I think they must have got there.

Lord, Liar, or Lunatic?

The following passage from *Mere Christianity*, (1) gives us "the key to history" with its record of repeated failure, (2) summarizes the four essential ingredients in religion (for an expanded version of this, see the whole Preface to *The Problem of Pain*, pp. 179ff.), and (3) presents a simple and shocking argument for the truth of the most radical claim any religion ever made: the Christian claim that this man was (and is!) *God*.

WHAT SATAN PUT INTO THE HEADS of our remote ancestors was the idea that they could "be like gods" —could set up on their own as if they had created themselves—be their own masters—invent some sort of happiness for themselves outside God, apart from God. And out of that hopeless attempt has come nearly all that we call human history—money, poverty, ambition, war, prostitution, classes, empires, slavery—the long terrible story of man trying to find something other than God which will make him happy.

The reason why it can never succeed is this. God made us: invented us as a man invents an engine. A car is made to run on gasoline, and it would not run properly on anything else. Now God designed the human machine to run on Himself. He Himself is the fuel our spirits were designed to burn, or the food our spirits were designed to feed on. There is no other. That is why it is just no good

Mere Christianity, pp. 53–56.

asking God to make us happy in our own way without bothering about religion. God cannot give us a happiness and peace apart from Himself, because it is not there. There is no such thing.

That is the key to history. Terrific energy is expended—civilisations are built up—excellent institutions devised; but each time something goes wrong. Some fatal flaw always brings the selfish and cruel people to the top and it all slides back into misery and ruin. In fact, the machine conks. It seems to start up all right and runs a few yards, and then it breaks down. They are trying to run it on the wrong juice. That is what Satan has done to us humans.

And what did God do? First of all He left us conscience, the sense of right and wrong: and all through history there have been people trying (some of them very hard) to obey it. None of them ever quite succeeded. Secondly, He sent the human race what I call good dreams: I mean those queer stories scattered all through the heathen religions about a god who dies and comes to life again and, by his death, has somehow given new life to men. Thirdly, He selected one particular people and spent several centuries hammering into their heads the sort of God He was—that there was only one of Him and that He cared about right conduct. Those people were the Jews, and the Old Testament gives an account of the hammering process.

Then comes the real shock. Among these Jews there suddenly turns up a man who goes about talking as if He was God. He claims to forgive sins. He says He has always existed. He says He is coming to judge the world at the end of time. Now let us get this clear. Among Pantheists, like the Indians, anyone might say that he was a part of God, or one with God: there would be nothing very odd about it. But this man, since He was a Jew, could not mean that kind of God. God, in their language, meant the Being outside the world Who had made it and was infinitely different from anything else. And when you have grasped that, you will see that what this man said was, quite simply, the most shocking thing that has ever been uttered by human lips.

One part of the claim tends to slip past us unnoticed because we have heard it so often that we no longer see what it amounts to. I mean the claim to forgive sins: any sins. Now unless the speaker is God, this is really so preposterous as to be comic. We can all understand how a man forgives offences against himself. You tread on my toe and I forgive you, you steal my money and I forgive you. But what should we make of a man, himself unrobbed and untrodden on, who announced that he forgave you for treading on other men's toes and stealing other men's money? Asinine fatuity is the kindest description we should give of his conduct. Yet this is what Jesus did. He told people that their sins were forgiven, and never waited to consult all the other people whom their sins had undoubtedly injured. He unhesitatingly behaved as if He was the party chiefly concerned, the person chiefly offended in all offences. This makes sense only if He really was the God whose laws are broken and whose love is wounded in every sin. In the mouth of any speaker who is not God, these words would imply what I can only regard as a silliness and conceit unrivalled by any other character in history.

Yet (and this is the strange, significant thing) even His enemies, when they read the Gospels, do not usually get the impression of silliness and conceit. Still less do un-prejudiced readers. Christ says that He is "humble and meek" and we believe Him; not noticing that, if He were merely a man, humility and meekness are the very last characteristics we could attribute to some of His sayings.

I am trying here to prevent anyone saying the really fool-ish thing that people often say about Him: "I'm ready to accept Jesus as the great moral teacher, but I don't accept His claim to be God." That is the one thing we must not say. A man who was merely a man and said the sort of things Jesus said would not be a great moral teacher. He would either be a lunatic—on a level with the man who says he is a poached egg—or else he would be the Devil of Hell. You must make your choice. Either this man was, and is, the Son of God: or else a madman or something worse. You can shut Him up for a fool, you can spit at Him and kill Him as a demon; or you can fall at His feet and call Him Lord and God. But let us not come with any patronising nonsense about His being a great human teacher. He has not left that open to us. He did not in-tend to.

"What Are We to Make of Jesus Christ?"

The argument for Christ's divinity at the end of the last reading is expanded in this short essay.

No one has ever refuted the argument. Few have even addressed it.

———————

WHAT ARE WE TO MAKE of Jesus Christ? This is a question which has, in a sense, a frantically comic side. For the real question is not what are we to make of Christ, but what is He to make of us? The picture of a fly sitting deciding what it is going to make of an elephant has comic elements about it. But perhaps the questioner meant what are we to make of Him in the sense of 'How are we to solve the historical problem set us by the recorded sayings and acts of this Man?' This problem is to reconcile two things. On the one hand you have got the almost generally admitted depth and sanity of His moral teaching, which is not very seriously questioned, even by those who are opposed to Christianity. In fact, I find when I am arguing with very anti-God people that they rather make a point of saying, 'I am entirely in favour of the moral teaching of Christianity'—and there seems to be a general agreement that in the teaching of this Man and of His immediate followers, moral truth is exhibited

God in the Dock, pp. 156–60.

at its purest and best. It is not sloppy idealism, it is full
of wisdom and shrewdness. The whole thing is realistic,
fresh to the highest degree, the product of a sane mind.
That is one phenomenon.

The other phenomenon is the quite appalling nature
of this Man's theological remarks. You all know what I
mean, and I want rather to stress the point that the appalling claim which this Man seems to be making is not
merely made at one moment of His career. There is, of
course, the one moment which led to His execution. The
moment at which the High Priest said to Him, 'Who
are you?' 'I am the Anointed, the Son of the uncreated
God, and you shall see Me appearing at the end of all
history as the judge of the Universe.' But that claim, in
fact, does not rest on this one dramatic moment. When
you look into His conversation you will find this sort of
claim running through the whole thing. For instance, He
went about saying to people, 'I forgive your sins.' Now
it is quite natural for a man to forgive something you do
to *him*. Thus if somebody cheats *me* out of £5 it is quite
possible and reasonable for me to say, 'Well, I forgive
him, we will say no more about it.' What on earth would
you say if somebody had done *you* out of £5 and *I* said,
'That is all right, I forgive him'? Then there is a curious
thing which seems to slip out almost by accident. On one
occasion this Man is sitting looking down on Jerusalem
from the hill above it and suddenly in comes an extraordi-
nary remark—'I keep on sending you prophets and wise
men.' Nobody comments on it. And yet, quite suddenly,
almost incidentally, He is claiming to be the power that
all through the centuries is sending wise men and leaders

into the world. Here is another curious remark: in almost every religion there are unpleasant observances like fasting. This Man suddenly remarks one day, 'No one need fast while I am here.' Who is this Man who remarks that His mere presence suspends all normal rules? Who is the person who can suddenly tell the School they can have a half-holiday? Sometimes the statements put forward the assumption that He, the Speaker, is completely without sin or fault. This is always the attitude. 'You, to whom I am talking, are all sinners,' and He never remotely suggests that this same reproach can be brought against Him. He says again, 'I am begotten of the One God, before Abraham was, I am,' and remember what the words 'I am' were in Hebrew. They were the name of God, which must not be spoken by any human being, the name which it was death to utter.

Well, that is the other side. On the one side clear, definite moral teaching. On the other, claims which, if not true, are those of a megalomaniac, compared with whom Hitler was the most sane and humble of men. There is no half-way house and there is no parallel in other religions. If you had gone to Buddha and asked him 'Are you the son of Bramah?' he would have said, 'My son, you are still in the vale of illusion.' If you had gone to Socrates and asked, 'Are you Zeus?' he would have laughed at you. If you had gone to Mohammed and asked, 'Are you Allah?' he would first have rent his clothes and then cut your head off. If you had asked Confucius, 'Are you Heaven?', I think he would have probably replied, 'Remarks which are not in accordance with nature are in bad taste.' The idea of a great moral teacher saying what Christ said is out of the question. In my opinion, the only person who can say that sort of thing is either God or a complete lunatic suffering from that form of delusion which undermines the whole mind of man. If you think you are a poached egg, when you are looking for a piece of toast to suit you, you may be sane, but if you think you are God, there is no chance for you. We may note in passing that He was never regarded as a mere moral teacher. He did not produce that effect on any of the people who actually met Him. He produced mainly three effects—Hatred —Terror—Adoration. There was no trace of people expressing mild approval.

What are we to do about reconciling the two contradictory phenomena? One attempt consists in saying that the Man did not really say these things, but that His followers exaggerated the story, and so the legend grew up that He had said them. This is difficult because His followers were all Jews; that is, they belonged to that Nation which of all others was most convinced that there was only one God —that there could not possibly be another. It is very odd that this horrible invention about a religious leader should grow up among the one people in the whole earth least likely to make such a mistake. On the contrary we get the impression that none of His immediate followers or even of the New Testament writers embraced the doctrine at all easily.

Another point is that on that view you would have to regard the accounts of the Man as being *legends*. Now, as a literary historian, I am perfectly convinced that whatever else the Gospels are they are not legends. I have read a great deal of legend and I am quite clear that they are not the same sort of thing. They are not artistic enough to be legends. From an imaginative point of view they are clumsy, they don't work up to things properly. Most of the life of Jesus is totally unknown to us, as is the life of anyone else who lived at that time, and no people building up a legend would allow that to be so. Apart from bits of the Platonic dialogues, there are no conversations that I know of in ancient literature like the Fourth Gospel. There is nothing, even in modern literature, until about a hundred years ago when the realistic novel came into existence. In the story of the woman taken in adultery we are told Christ bent down and scribbled in the dust with His finger. Nothing comes of this. No one has ever based any doctrine on it. And the art of *inventing* little irrelevant details to make an imaginary scene more convincing is a purely modern art. Surely the only explanation of this passage is that the thing really happened? The author put it in simply because he had *seen* it.

Then we come to the strangest story of all, the story of the Resurrection. It is very necessary to get the story clear. I heard a man say, 'The importance of the Resurrection is that it gives evidence of survival, evidence that the human personality survives death.' On that view what happened to Christ would be what had always happened to all men, the difference being that in Christ's case we were privileged to see it happening. This is certainly not what the earliest Christian writers thought. Something perfectly new in the history of the Universe had happened. Christ had defeated death. The door which had always been locked had for the very first time been forced open. This is something quite distinct from mere ghost-survival. I don't mean that they disbelieved in ghost-survival. On the contrary, they believed in it so firmly that, on more than one occasion, Christ had had to assure them that He was *not* a ghost. The point is that while believing in survival they yet regarded the Resurrection as something totally different and new. The Resurrection narratives are not a picture of survival after death; they record how a totally new mode of being has arisen in the Universe. Something new had appeared in the Universe: as new as the first coming of organic life. This Man, after death, does not get divided into 'ghost' and 'corpse'. A new mode of being has arisen. That is the story. What are we going to make of it?

The question is, I suppose, whether any hypothesis covers the facts so well as the Christian hypothesis. That hypothesis is that God has come down into the created universe, down to manhood—and come up again, pulling it up with Him. The alternative hypothesis is not legend, nor exaggeration, nor the apparitions of a ghost. It is either lunacy or lies. Unless one can take the second alternative (and I can't) one turns to the Christian theory.

'What are we to make of Christ?' There is no question of what we can make of Him, it is entirely a question of what He intends to make of us. You must accept or reject the story.

The things He says are very different from what any other teacher has said. Others say, 'This is the truth about the Universe. This is the way you ought to go,' but He says, '*I* am the Truth, and the Way, and the Life.' He says, 'No man can reach absolute reality, except through Me. Try to retain your own life and you will be inevitably ruined. Give yourself away and you will be saved.' He says, 'If you are ashamed of Me, if, when you hear this call, you turn the other way, I also will look the other way when I come again as God without disguise. If anything whatever is keeping you from God and from Me, whatever it is, throw it away. If it is your eye, pull it out. If it is your hand, cut it off. If you put yourself first you will be last. Come to Me everyone who is carrying a heavy load, I will set that right. Your sins, all of them, are wiped out, I can do that. I am Re-birth, I am Life. Eat Me, drink Me, I am your Food. And finally, do not be afraid, I have overcome the whole Universe.' That is the issue.

The Lamb and the Lion

At the end of *The Voyage of the Dawn Treader*, Lucy and her companions have come from earth into Narnia by magic (in *The Lion, the Witch and the Wardrobe* it was through a wardrobe; in this book it is through a picture); have found the spatial "end of the world" (Narnia is flat) by sailing to "the utter East", searching for Aslan's country; and now meet Aslan as both Lamb and Lion. He tells them how to get to his country from their own world (earth), and why they were brought to Narnia by Aslan—and why we were brought to Narnia by Lewis.

"PLEASE, LAMB," said Lucy, "is this the way to Aslan's country?"

"Not for you," said the Lamb. "For you the door into Aslan's country is from your own world."

"What!" said Edmund. "Is there a way into Aslan's country from our world too?"

"There is a way into my country from all the worlds," said the Lamb; but as he spoke his snowy white flushed into tawny gold and his size changed and he was Aslan himself, towering above them and scattering light from his mane.

"Oh, Aslan," said Lucy. "Will you tell us how to get into your country from our world?"

The Voyage of the Dawn Treader, pp. 208–9.

"I shall be telling you all the time," said Aslan. "But I will not tell you how long or short the way will be; only that it lies across a river. But do not fear that, for I am the great Bridge Builder. And now come; I will open the door in the sky and send you to your own land."

"Please, Aslan," said Lucy. "Before we go, will you tell us when we can come back to Narnia again? Please. And oh, do, do, do make it soon."

"Dearest," said Aslan very gently, "you and your brother will never come back to Narnia."

"Oh, *Aslan*!" said Edmund and Lucy both together in despairing voices.

"You are too old, children," said Aslan, "and you must begin to come close to your own world now."

"It isn't Narnia, you know," sobbed Lucy. "It's *you*. We shan't meet *you* there. And how can we live, never meeting you?"

"But you shall meet me, dear one," said Aslan.

"Are—are you there too, Sir?" said Edmund.

"I am," said Aslan. "But there I have another name. You must learn to know me by that name. This was the very reason why you were brought to Narnia, that by knowing me here for a little, you may know me better there."

"They Went All Trembly"

What is it like to meet Aslan? What is it like to know Christ? The two following short passages tell us. It is "to go all trembly". In Rabbi Abraham Heschel's words, "God is not an uncle. God is an earthquake." (If your teachers tell you otherwise, that proves they have never *met* Him.)

"THEY SAY ASLAN IS ON THE MOVE—perhaps has already landed."

And now a very curious thing happened. None of the children knew who Aslan was any more than you do; but the moment the Beaver had spoken these words everyone felt quite different. Perhaps it has sometimes happened to you in a dream that someone says something which you don't understand but in the dream it feels as if it had some enormous meaning—either a terrifying one which turns the whole dream into a nightmare or else a lovely meaning —too lovely to put into words, which makes the dream so beautiful that you remember it all your life and are always wishing you could get into that dream again. It was like that now. At the name of Aslan each one of the children felt something jump in his inside. Edmund felt a sensation of mysterious horror. Peter felt suddenly brave and adventurous. Susan felt as if some delicious smell or some delightful strain of music had just floated by her.

The Lion, the Witch and the Wardrobe, pp. 54–55, 103.

And Lucy got the feeling you have when you wake up in the morning and realise that it is the beginning of the holidays or the beginning of summer. . . .

People who have not been in Narnia sometimes think that a thing cannot be good and terrible at the same time. If the children had ever thought so, they were cured of it now. For when they tried to look at Aslan's face they just caught a glimpse of the golden mane and the great, royal, solemn, overwhelming eyes; and then they found they couldn't look at him and went all trembly.

V

THE PROBLEM OF PAIN

"Experience is a brutal teacher. But you learn. By God, you learn."

"When it gets close, you find out whether you really believe or not."

"I'm not sure God wants us to be happy. He wants us to grow up—to love."

— *"Shadowlands"* (the movie)

"The Problem of Pain"

Is CHRISTIANITY a "warm, fuzzy theology", as one critic of *Shadowlands*' sympathetic treatment of Lewis complained? Doesn't the brute fact of pain, especially the pains suffered by good people, give the lie to the whole previous picture this book has painted and prove it is sheer fantasy and escapism?

No. It *tests* faith, it does not *refute* it. C. S. Lewis had his faith sorely tested by his wife's death, but he did not lose it, as many viewers interpreted the movie to imply. What really happened was recorded in his diary in *A Grief Observed*.

Nor was his earlier theology of suffering a set of shallow clichés or easy answers, as many viewers also interpreted the movie to imply. You can see this for yourself in the excerpts from *The Problem of Pain*—the most rational answer I know to the most mysterious puzzle in life.

But the experience of suffering certainly deepened Lewis' wisdom and love, as it did Job's. (Why else would God allow it? It was deep and bloody heart surgery. But not all the spilt blood was Lewis'. This Surgeon operates from a Cross.)

Explaining Pain

The beginning of the following reading, the Preface to *The Problem of Pain*, shows that Lewis was refreshingly free from arrogance, hypocrisy, stuffiness and puffery even before marriage and bereavement taught him deeper experiential wisdom through suffering.

The third paragraph (p. 180) summarizes the essence of the problem and the solution from a logical point of view.

The samples that follow are only a few pearls along the thread of the argument.

Preface

WHEN MR ASHLEY SAMPSON suggested to me the writing of this book, I asked leave to be allowed to write it anonymously, since, if I were to say what I really thought about pain, I should be forced to make statements of such apparent fortitude that they would become ridiculous if anyone knew who made them. Anonymity was rejected as inconsistent with the series; but Mr Sampson pointed out that I could write a preface explaining that I did not live up to my own principles! This exhilarating programme I am now carrying out. . . . The only purpose of the book is to solve the intellectual problem raised by suffering; for the far higher task of teaching fortitude and patience I was never fool enough to suppose

The Problem of Pain, pp. 9–10, 83–84, 32–33, 44, 71, 74, 76–78, 92.

myself qualified, nor have I anything to offer my readers except my conviction that when pain is to be borne, a little courage helps more than much knowledge, a little human sympathy more than much courage, and the least tincture of the love of God more than all. . . .

All arguments in justification of suffering provoke bitter resentment against the author. You would like to know how I behave when I am experiencing pain, not writing books about it. You need not guess, for I will tell you; I am a great coward. . . .

"If God were good, He would wish to make His creatures perfectly happy, and if God were almighty He would be able to do what He wished. But the creatures are not happy. Therefore God lacks either goodness, or power, or both." This is the problem of pain, in its simplest form. The possibility of answering it depends on showing that the terms "good" and "almighty", and perhaps also the term "happy", are equivocal: for it must be admitted from the outset that if the popular meanings attached to these words are the best, or the only possible, meanings, then the argument is unanswerable. . . .

Omnipotence

His Omnipotence means power to do all that is intrinsically possible, not to do the intrinsically impossible. You may attribute miracles to Him, but not nonsense. This is no limit to His power. If you choose to say "God can give a creature free-will and at the same time withhold free-will from it", you have not succeeded in saying *anything* about God: meaningless combinations of words do not suddenly acquire meaning simply because we prefix to them the two other words "God can". It remains true that all *things* are possible with God: the intrinsic impossibilities are not things but nonentities. It is no more possible for God than for the weakest of His creatures to carry out both of two mutually exclusive alternatives; not because His power meets an obstacle, but because nonsense remains nonsense even when we talk it about God.

It should, however, be remembered that human reasoners often make mistakes, either by arguing from false data or by inadvertence in the argument itself. We may thus come to think things possible which are really impossible, and *vice versa*. We ought, therefore, to use great caution in defining those intrinsic impossibilities which even Omnipotence cannot perform. What follows is to be regarded less as an assertion of what they are than a sample of what they might be like.

The inexorable "laws of Nature" which operate in defiance of human suffering or desert, which are not turned aside by prayer, seem, at first sight, to furnish a strong argument against the goodness and power of God. I am going to submit that not even Omnipotence could create a society of free souls without at the same time creating a relatively independent and "inexorable" Nature. . . .

Again, the freedom of a creature must mean freedom to choose: and choice implies the existence of things to choose between. A creature with no environment would have no choices to make. . . .

Society, then, implies a common field or "world" in which its members meet. . . .

But if matter is to serve as a neutral field it must have a fixed nature of its own. . . .

Again, if matter has a fixed nature and obeys constant laws, not all states of matter will be equally agreeable to the wishes of a given soul, nor all equally beneficial for that particular aggregate of matter which he calls his body. . . .

The permanent nature of wood which enables us to use it as a beam also enables us to use it for hitting our neighbour on the head. The permanent nature of matter in general means that when human beings fight, the victory ordinarily goes to those who have superior weapons, skill, and numbers, even if their cause is unjust.

We can, perhaps, conceive of a world in which God corrected the results of this abuse of free-will by His creatures at every moment: so that a wooden beam became soft as grass when it was used as a weapon, and the air refused to obey me if I attempted to set up in it the sound-waves that carry lies or insults. But such a world would be one in which wrong actions were impossible, and in which, therefore, freedom of the will would be void; nay, if the principle were carried out to its logical conclusion, evil thoughts would be impossible, for the cerebral matter which we use in thinking would refuse its task when we attempted to frame them. All matter in the neighbour-hood of a wicked man would be liable to undergo un-predictable alterations. That God can and does, on occasions, modify the behaviour of matter and produce what we call miracles, is part of Christian faith; but the very conception of a common, and therefore stable, world, demands that these occasions should be extremely rare. In a game of chess you can make certain arbitrary concessions to your opponent, which stand to the ordinary rules of the game as miracles stand to the laws of nature. You can deprive yourself of a castle, or allow the other man sometimes to take back a move made inadvertently. But if you conceded everything that at any moment happened to suit him—if all his moves were revocable and if all your pieces disappeared whenever their position on the board was not to his liking—then you could not have a game at all. So it is with the life of souls in a world: fixed laws, consequences unfolding by causal necessity, the whole natural order, are at once limits within which their common life is confined and also the sole condition under which any such life is possible. Try to exclude the possibility of suffering which the order of nature and the existence of free-wills involve, and you find that you have excluded life itself. . . .

Goodness

By the goodness of God we mean nowadays almost exclusively His lovingness; and in this we may be right. And by Love, in this context, most of us mean kindness —the desire to see others than the self happy; not happy in this way or in that, but just happy. What would really satisfy us would be a God who said of anything we happened to like doing, "What does it matter so long as they are contented?" We want, in fact, not so much a Father in Heaven as a grandfather in heaven—a senile benevo-

lence who, as they say, "liked to see young people enjoying themselves" and whose plan for the universe was
simply that it might be truly said at the end of each day,
"a good time was had by all". Not many people, I admit,
would formulate a theology in precisely those terms: but
a conception not very different lurks at the back of many
minds. I do not claim to be an exception: I should very
much like to live in a universe which was governed on
such lines. But since it is abundantly clear that I don't,
and since I have reason to believe, nevertheless, that God
is Love, I conclude that my conception of love needs cor-
rection.

I might, indeed, have learned, even from the poets,
that Love is something more stern and splendid than mere
kindness: that even the love between the sexes is, as in
Dante, "a lord of terrible aspect". There is kindness in
Love: but Love and kindness are not coterminous, and
when kindness (in the sense given above) is separated
from the other elements of Love, it involves a certain
fundamental indifference to its object, and even something like contempt of it. Kindness consents very read-
ily to the removal of its object—we have all met people whose kindness to animals is constantly leading them
to kill animals lest they should suffer. Kindness, merely
as such, cares not whether its object becomes good or
bad, provided only that it escapes suffering. As Scripture
points out, it is bastards who are spoiled: the legitimate
sons, who are to carry on the family tradition, are punished (Heb 12:5–8). It is for people whom we care nothing about that we demand happiness on any terms: with
our friends, our lovers, our children, we are exacting and

would rather see them suffer much than be happy in contemptible and estranging modes. If God is Love, He is, by definition, something more than mere kindness. And it appears, from all the records, that though He has often rebuked us and condemned us, He has never regarded us with contempt. He has paid us the intolerable compliment of loving us, in the deepest, most tragic, most inexorable sense. . . .

Human Wickedness

The examples given in the last chapter went to show that love may cause pain to its object, but only on the supposition that that object needs alteration to become fully lovable. Now why do we men need so much alteration? The Christian answer—that we have used our free will to become very bad—is so well known that it hardly needs to be stated. But to bring this doctrine into real life in the minds of modern men, and even of modern Christians, is very hard. When the apostles preached, they could assume even in their Pagan hearers a real consciousness of deserving the Divine anger. The Pagan mysteries existed to allay this consciousness, and the Epicurean philosophy claimed to deliver men from the fear of eternal punishment. It was against this background that the Gospel appeared as good news. It brought news of possible healing to men who knew that they were mortally ill. But all this has changed. Christianity now has to preach the diagnosis—in itself very bad news—before it can win a hearing for the cure. . . .

I have tried to show in a previous chapter that the possibility of pain is inherent in the very existence of a world where souls can meet. When souls become wicked they will certainly use this possibility to hurt one another; and this, perhaps, accounts for four-fifths of the sufferings of men. It is men, not God, who have produced racks, whips, prisons, slavery, guns, bayonets, and bombs; it is by human avarice or human stupidity, not by the churlishness of nature, that we have poverty and overwork. But there remains, none the less, much suffering which cannot thus be traced to ourselves. . . .

Pain is not only immediately recognisable evil, but evil impossible to ignore. We can rest contentedly in our sins and in our stupidities; and anyone who has watched gluttons shovelling down the most exquisite foods as if they did not know what they were eating, will admit that we can ignore even pleasure. But pain insists upon being attended to. God whispers to us in our pleasures, speaks in our conscience, but shouts in our pain: it is His megaphone to rouse a deaf world. A bad man, happy, is a man without the least inkling that his actions do not "answer", that they are not in accord with the laws of the universe. . . .

If the first and lowest operation of pain shatters the illusion that all is well, the second shatters the illusion that what we have, whether good or bad in itself, is our own and enough for us. Everyone has noticed how hard it is to turn our thoughts to God when everything is going well with us. We "have all we want" is a terrible saying when "all" does not include God. We find God an interruption. As St Augustine says somewhere, "God wants to give us something, but cannot, because our hands are full—there's nowhere for Him to put it." Or as a friend of mine said, "We regard God as an airman regards his parachute; it's there for emergencies but he hopes he'll never have to use it." Now God, who has made us, knows what we are and that our happiness lies in Him. Yet we will not seek it in Him as long as He leaves us any other resort where it can even plausibly be looked for. While what we call "our own life" remains agreeable we will not surrender it to Him. What then can God do in our interests but make "our own life" less agreeable to us, and take away the plausible source of false happiness? It is just here, where God's providence seems at first to be most cruel, that the Divine humility, the stooping down of the Highest, most deserves praise. We are perplexed to see misfortune falling upon decent, inoffensive, worthy people—on capable, hard-working mothers of families or diligent, thrifty, little trades-people, on those who have worked so hard, and so honestly, for their modest stock of happiness and now seem to be entering on the enjoyment of it with the fullest right. How can I say with sufficient tenderness what here needs to be said? It does not matter that I know I must become, in the eyes of every hostile reader, as it were personally responsible for all the sufferings I try to explain—just as, to this day, everyone talks as if St Augustine *wanted* unbaptised infants to go to Hell. But it matters enormously if I alienate anyone from the truth. Let me implore the reader to try to believe, if only for the moment, that God, who made these deserving people, may really be right when He thinks that their modest prosperity and the happiness of their children are not enough to make them blessed: that all this must fall from them in the end, and that if they have not learned to know Him they will be wretched. And therefore He troubles them, warning them in advance of an insufficiency that one day they will have to discover. The life to themselves and their families stands between them and the recognition of their need; He makes that life less sweet to them. I call this a Divine humility because it is a poor thing to strike our colours to God when the ship is going down under us; a poor thing to come to Him as a last resort, to offer up "our own" when it is no longer worth keeping. If God were proud He would hardly have us on such terms: but He is not proud, He stoops to conquer, He will have us even though we have shown that we prefer everything else to Him, and come to Him because there is "nothing better" now to be had. The same humility is shown by all those Divine appeals to our fears which trouble high-minded readers of Scripture. It is hardly complimentary to God that we should choose Him as an alternative to Hell: yet even this He accepts. The creature's illusion of self-sufficiency must, for the creature's sake, be shattered; and by trouble or fear of trouble on earth, by crude fear of the eternal flames, God shatters it "unmindful of His glory's diminution". Those who would like the God of Scripture to be more purely ethical, do not know what they ask. If God were a Kantian, who would not have us till we came to Him from the purest and best motives, who could be saved? And this illusion of self-sufficiency may be at its strongest in some very honest, kindly, and temperate people, and on such people, therefore, misfortune must fall.

The dangers of apparent self-sufficiency explain why Our Lord regards the vices of the feckless and dissipated so much more leniently than the vices that lead to worldly success. Prostitutes are in no danger of finding their present life so satisfactory that they cannot turn to God: the proud, the avaricious, the self-righteous, are in that danger. . . .

❦

The Christian doctrine of suffering explains, I believe, a very curious fact about the world we live in. The settled happiness and security which we all desire, God withholds from us by the very nature of the world: but joy, pleasure, and merriment, He has scattered broadcast. We are never safe, but we have plenty of fun, and some ecstasy. It is not hard to see why. The security we crave would teach us to rest our hearts in this world and oppose an obstacle to our return to God: a few moments of happy love, a landscape, a symphony, a merry meeting with our friends, a bathe or a football match, have no such tendency. Our Father refreshes us on the journey with some pleasant inns, but will not encourage us to mistake them for home.

Experiencing Pain

In *The Problem of Pain* Lewis does not *intend* to address the psychological but only the logical aspects of the problem. In *A Grief Observed* he does not intend to solve the problem logically. There is no *contradiction*, but a great *difference*, between the two books, as between the two parts of Lewis' adult life.

I have divided the excerpts from *A Grief Observed* into four themes:

    1. The experience of the pain of Joy's death;

    2. The problem this raises about whether God is good and how Lewis addressed this problem from the crucible of his suffering. (Note here especially how reason and faith work as allies, not enemies, against foolishness and despair.);

    3. Lewis' honest introspective questioning of his own faith (Faith does not stifle questioning!); and

    4. How love proved stronger than death; how Lewis "met" the essential Joy again after death.

The ultimate answer to all the great questions lies in the last sentence (p. 201). It is the same thing all the mystics say.

---

1. *The Pain*

IT IS HARD TO HAVE PATIENCE with people who say, "There is no death," or, "Death doesn't matter." There is death. And whatever is matters. And whatever

A Grief Observed (New York: Seabury Press, 1961), pp. 16, 11, 40–41, 67, 4–5, 33–36, 49–51, 84–85, 56–59, 76–77, 41, 43–45, 79–82, 32–33, 73–74, 85–88, 83.

happens has consequences, and it and they are irrevocable and irreversible. You might as well say that birth doesn't matter. I look up at the night sky. Is anything more certain than that in all those vast times and spaces, if I were allowed to search them, I should nowhere find her face, her voice, her touch? She died. She is dead. Is the word so difficult to learn?. . . .

Her absence is like the sky, spread over everything. . . .

There is spread over everything a vague sense of wrongness, of something amiss. Like in those dreams where nothing terrible occurs—nothing that would sound even remarkable if you told it at breakfast-time—but the atmosphere, the taste, of the whole thing is deadly. So with this. I see the rowan berries reddening and don't know for a moment why they, of all things, should be depressing. I hear a clock strike and some quality it always had before has gone out of the sound. What's wrong with the world to make it so flat, shabby, worn-out looking? then I remember. . . .

How often—will it be for always?—how often will the vast emptiness astonish me like a complete novelty and make me say, "I never realized my loss till this moment"? The same leg is cut off time after time. The first plunge of the knife into the flesh is felt again and again.

They say "The coward dies many times;" so does the beloved. . . .

2. God

Meanwhile, where is God? This is one of the most disquieting symptoms. When you are happy, so happy that you have no sense of needing Him, so happy that you are tempted to feel His claims upon you as an interruption, if you remember yourself and turn to Him with gratitude and praise, you will be—or so it feels—welcomed with open arms. But go to Him when your need is desperate, when all other help is vain, and what do you find? A door slammed in your face, and a sound of bolting and double bolting on the inside. After that, silence. . . .

I tried to put some of these thoughts to C. this afternoon. He reminded me that the same thing seems to have happened to Christ: "Why hast thou forsaken me?" I know. Does that make it easier to understand?

Not that I am (I think) in much danger of ceasing to believe in God. The real danger is of coming to believe such dreadful things about Him. The conclusion I dread is not, "So there's no God after all," but, "So this is what God's really like. Deceive yourself no longer.". . .

Sooner or later I must face the question in plain language. What reason have we, except our own desperate wishes, to believe that God is, by any standard we can conceive, "good"? Doesn't all the *prima facie* evidence suggest exactly the opposite? What have we to set against it?

We set Christ against it. But how if He were mistaken? Almost His last words may have a perfectly clear meaning. He had found that the Being He called Father was horribly and infinitely different from what He had supposed. The trap, so long and carefully prepared and so subtly baited, was at last sprung, on the cross. The vile practical joke had succeeded. . . .

I wrote that last night. It was a yell rather than a thought. Let me try it over again. Is it rational to believe in a bad God? Anyway, in a God so bad as all that? The Cosmic Sadist, the spiteful imbecile?

I think it is, if nothing else, too anthropomorphic. When you come to think of it, it is far more anthropomorphic than picturing Him as a grave old king with a long beard. That image is a Jungian archetype. It links God with all the wise old kings in the fairy tales, with prophets, sages, magicians. Though it is (formally) the picture of a man, it suggests something more than humanity. At the very least it gets in the idea of something older than yourself, something that knows more, something you can't fathom. It preserves mystery. Therefore room for hope. Therefore room for a dread or awe that needn't be mere fear of mischief from a spiteful potentate. But the picture I was building up last night is simply the picture of a man like S. C.—who used to sit next to me at dinner and tell me what he'd been doing to the cats that afternoon. Now a being like S. C., however magnified, couldn't invent or create or govern anything. He would set traps and try to bait them. But he'd never have thought of baits like love, or laughter, or daffodils, or a frosty sunset. *He* make a universe? He couldn't make a joke, or a bow, or an apology, or a friend. . . .

The terrible thing is that a perfectly good God is in this matter hardly less formidable than a Cosmic Sadist. The more we believe that God hurts only to heal, the less we can believe that there is any use in begging for tenderness. A cruel man might be bribed—might grow tired of his vile sport—might have a temporary fit of mercy, as alcoholics have fits of sobriety. But suppose that what you are up against is a surgeon whose intentions are wholly good. The kinder and more conscientious he is, the more inexorably he will go on cutting. If he yielded to your entreaties, if he stopped before the operation was complete, all the pain up to that point would have been useless. But is it credible that such extremities of torture should be necessary for us? Well, take your choice. The tortures occur. If they are unnecessary, then there is no God or a bad one. If there is a good God, then these tortures are necessary. For no even moderately good Being could possibly inflict or permit them if they weren't.

Either way, we're for it.

What do people mean when they say, "I am not afraid of God because I know He is good?" Have they never even been to a dentist? . . .

Sometimes, Lord, one is tempted to say that if you wanted us to behave like the lilies of the field you might have given us an organization more like theirs. . . . To make an organism which is also a spirit; to make that terrible oxymoron, a "spiritual animal." To take a poor primate, a beast with nerve-endings all over it, a creature with a stomach that wants to be filled, a breeding animal that wants its mate, and say, "Now get on with it. Become a god." . . .

"It was too perfect to last," so I am tempted to say of our marriage. But it can be meant in two ways. It may be grimly pessimistic—as if God no sooner saw two of His creatures happy than He stopped it ("None of that here!"). As if He were like the Hostess at the sherry-party who separates two guests the moment they show signs of having got into a real conversation. But it could also mean "This had reached its proper perfection. This had become what it had in it to be. Therefore of course it would not be prolonged." As if God said, "Good; you have mastered that exercise. I am very pleased with it. And now you are ready to go on to the next." When you have learned to do quadratics and enjoy doing them you will not be set them much longer. The teacher moves you on. . . .

❧

And then one or other dies. And we think of this as love cut short; like a dance stopped in mid-career or a flower with its head unluckily snapped off—something truncated and therefore, lacking its due shape. I wonder. If, as I can't help suspecting, the dead also feel the pains of separation (and this may be one of their purgatorial sufferings), then for both lovers, and for all pairs of lovers without exception, bereavement is a universal and integral part of our experience of love. It follows marriage as normally as marriage follows courtship or as autumn follows summer. It is not a truncation of the process but one of its phases; not the interruption of the dance, but the next figure. We are "taken out of ourselves" by the loved one while she is here. Then comes the tragic figure of the dance in which we must learn to be still taken out of ourselves though the bodily presence is withdrawn, to love the very Her, and not fall back to loving our past, or our memory, or our sorrow, or our relief from sorrow, or our own love. . . .

My idea of God is not a divine idea. It has to be shattered time after time. He shatters it Himself. He is the great iconoclast. Could we not almost say that this shattering is one of the marks of His presence? The Incarnation is the supreme example; it leaves all previous ideas of the Messiah in ruins. And most are "offended" by the iconoclasm; and blessed are those who are not. But the same thing happens in our private prayers.

All reality is iconoclastic. The earthly beloved, even in this life, incessantly triumphs over your mere idea of her. And you want her to; you want her with all her resistances, all her faults, all her unexpectedness. That is, in her foursquare and independent reality. And this, not any image or memory, is what we are to love still, after she is dead. . . .

3. Self-doubt

Feelings, and feelings, and feelings. Let me try thinking instead. From the rational point of view, what new factor has H.'s death introduced into the problem of the universe? What grounds has it given me for doubting all that I believe? I knew already that these things, and worse, happened daily. . . .

Bridge-players tell me that there must be some money on the game, "or else people won't take it seriously." Apparently it's like that. Your bid—for God or no God, for a good God or the Cosmic Sadist, for eternal life or nonentity—will not be serious if nothing much is staked on it. And you will never discover how serious it was until the stakes are raised horribly high; until you find that you are playing not for counters or for sixpences but for every penny you have in the world. Nothing less will shake a man—or at any rate a man like me—out of his merely verbal thinking and his merely notional beliefs. He has to be knocked silly before he comes to his senses. Only torture will bring out the truth. Only under torture does he discover it himself.

And I must surely admit—H. would have forced me to admit in a few passes—that, if my house was a house of cards, the sooner it was knocked down the better. And only suffering could do it. But then the Cosmic Sadist and Eternal Vivisector becomes an unnecessary hypothesis. . . .

Indeed it's likely enough that what I shall call, if it happens, a "restoration of faith" will turn out to be only one more house of cards. And I shan't know whether it is or not until the next blow comes—when, say, fatal disease is diagnosed in my body too, or war breaks out, or I have ruined myself by some ghastly mistake in my work. But there are two questions here. In which sense may it be a house of cards? Because the things I am believing are only a dream, or because I only dream that I believe them? . . .

Am I, for instance, just sidling back to God because I know that if there's any road to H., it runs through Him? But then of course I know perfectly well that He can't be used as a road. If you're approaching Him not as the goal but as a road, not as the end but as a means, you're not really approaching Him at all. That's what was really wrong with all those popular pictures of happy reunions "on the further shore;" not the simple-minded and very earthly images, but the fact that they make an End of what we can get only as a by-product of the true End.

Lord, are these your real terms? Can I meet H. again only if I learn to love you so much that I don't care whether I meet her or not? Consider, Lord, how it looks to us. What would anyone think of me if I said to the boys, "No toffee now. But when you've grown up and don't really want toffee you shall have as much of it as you choose?" . . .

And now that I come to think of it, there's no practical problem before me at all. I know the two great commandments, and I'd better get on with them. Indeed, H.'s death has ended the practical problem. While she was alive I could, in practice, have put her before God; that is, could have done what she wanted instead of what He wanted; if there'd been a conflict. What's left is not a problem about anything I could *do*. It's all about weights of feelings and motives and that sort of thing. It's a problem I'm setting myself. I don't believe God set it me at all. . . .

4. Love is stronger than death

If H. "is not," then she never was. I mistook a cloud of atoms for a person. There aren't, and never were, any people. Death only reveals the vacuity that was always there. What we call the living are simply those who have not yet been unmasked. All equally bankrupt, but some not yet declared. But this must be nonsense; vacuity revealed to whom? bankruptcy declared to whom? To other boxes of fireworks or clouds of atoms. I will never believe —more strictly I can't believe—that one set of physical events could be, or make, a mistake about other sets. . . .

One moment last night can be described in similes; otherwise it won't go into language at all. Imagine a man in total darkness. He thinks he is in a cellar or dungeon. Then there comes a sound. He thinks it might be a sound from far off—waves or wind-blown trees or cattle half a mile away. And if so, it proves he's not in a cellar, but free, in the open air. Or it may be a much smaller sound close at hand—a chuckle of laughter. And if so, there is a friend just beside him in the dark. Either way, a good, good sound. . . .

❦

I said, several notebooks ago, that even if I got what seemed like an assurance of H.'s presence, I wouldn't believe it. Easier said than done. Even now, though, I won't treat anything of that sort as evidence. It's the *quality* of last night's experience—not what it proves but what it was—that makes it worth putting down. It was quite incredibly unemotional. Just the impression of her *mind* momentarily facing my own. Mind, not "soul" as we tend to think of soul. Certainly the reverse of what is called "soulful." Not at all like a rapturous reunion of lovers. Much more like getting a telephone call or a wire from her about some practical arrangement. Not that there was any "message"—just intelligence and attention. No sense of joy or sorrow. No love even, in our ordinary sense. No un-love. I had never in any mood imagined the dead as being so—well, so business-like. Yet there was an extreme and cheerful intimacy. An intimacy that had not passed through the senses or the emotions at all.

If this was a throw-up from my unconscious, then my unconscious must be a far more interesting region than the depth psychologists have led me to expect. For one thing, it is apparently much less primitive than my consciousness.

Wherever it came from, it has made a sort of spring cleaning in my mind. The dead could be like that; sheer intellects. A Greek philosopher wouldn't have been surprised at an experience like mine. He would have expected that if anything of us remained after death it would be just that. Up to now this always seemed to me a most arid and chilling idea. The absence of emotion repelled me. But in this contact (whether real or apparent) it didn't do anything of the sort. One didn't need emotion. The intimacy was complete—sharply bracing and restorative too—without it. Can that intimacy be love itself—always in this life attended with emotion, not because it is itself an emotion, or needs an attendant emotion, but because our animal souls, our nervous systems, our imaginations, have to respond to it in that way? If so, how many preconceptions I must scrap! A society, a communion, of pure intelligences would not be cold, drab and comfortless. On the other hand it wouldn't be very like what people usually mean when they use such words as "spiritual," or "mystical," or "holy." It would, if I have had a glimpse, be—well, I'm almost scared at the adjectives I'd have to use. Brisk? cheerful? keen? alert? intense? wide-awake? Above all, solid. Utterly reliable. Firm. There is no nonsense about the dead.

When I say "intellect" I include will. Attention is an act of will. Intelligence in action is will *par excellence*. What seemed to meet me was full of resolution. . . .

Heaven will solve our problems, but not, I think, by showing us subtle reconciliations between all our apparently contradictory notions. The notions will all be knocked from under our feet. We shall see that there never was any problem.

And, more than once, that impression which I can't describe except by saying that it's like the sound of a chuckle in the darkness. The sense that some shattering and disarming simplicity is the real answer.

"Footnote to All Prayers"

The two poems that follow refute the popular piece of bigotry that assumes that orthodox Christians are bigoted, that if you believe the Christian dogma *you* must be "dogmatic".

―――――――――

HE WHOM I BOW TO only knows to whom I bow
  When I attempt the ineffable Name, murmuring
    Thou,
And dream of Pheidian fancies and embrace in heart
Symbols (I know) which cannot be the thing Thou
    art.
Thus always, taken at their word, all prayers
    blaspheme
Worshipping with frail images a folk-lore dream,
And all men in their praying, self-deceived, address
The coinage of their own unquiet thoughts, unless
Thou in magnetic mercy to Thyself divert
Our arrows, aimed unskilfully, beyond desert;
And all men are idolators, crying unheard
To a deaf idol, if Thou take them at their word.

Take not, oh Lord, our literal sense. Lord, in Thy
    great,
Unbroken speech our limping metaphor translate.

Poems, p. 129.

"The Apologist's Evening Prayer"

F ROM ALL MY LAME DEFEATS and oh! much more
From all the victories that I seemed to score;
From cleverness shot forth on Thy behalf
At which, while angels weep, the audience laugh;
From all my proofs of Thy divinity,
Thou, who wouldst give no sign, deliver me.

Thoughts are but coins. Let me not trust, instead
Of Thee, their thin-worn image of Thy head.
From all my thoughts, even from my thoughts
    of Thee,
O thou fair Silence, fall, and set me free.
Lord of the narrow gate and the needle's eye,
Take from me all my trumpery lest I die.

Poems, p. 129.

"No Earthly Comfort"

The poem and two following readings display the hard truth that Lewis always *believed*, but *tasted* only because of Joy: that to love is to suffer; that God is not a spiritual aspirin to relieve suffering; that Christianity is not a warm fuzzy fairy tale.

————————

O<small>F THIS WE'RE CERTAIN</small>; no one who dared knock
  At heaven's door for earthly comfort found
Even a door—only smooth, endless rock,
And save the echo of his cry no sound.
It's dangerous to listen; you'll begin
To fancy that those echoes (hope can play
Pitiful tricks) are answers from within;
Far better to turn, grimly sane, away.
Heaven cannot thus, Earth cannot ever, give
The thing we want. We ask what isn't there
And by our asking water and make live
That very part of love which must despair
And die and go down cold into the earth
Before there's talk of springtime and re-birth.

Pitch your demands heaven-high and they'll be met.
Ask for the Morning Star and take (thrown in)
Your earthly love. Why, yes; but how to set
One's foot on the first rung, how to begin?

Poems, pp. 126–27, "Five Sonnets", nos. 3–5.

The silence of one voice upon our ears
Beats like the waves; the coloured morning seems
A lying brag; the face we loved appears
Fainter each night, or ghastlier, in our dreams.
'That long way round which Dante trod was meant
For mighty saints and mystics not for me,'
So Nature cries. Yet if we once assent
To Nature's voice, we shall be like the bee
That booms against the window-pane for hours
Thinking that way to reach the laden flowers.

'If we could speak to her,' my doctor said,
'And told her, "Not that way! All, all in vain
You weary out your wings and bruise your head,"
Might she not answer, buzzing at the pane,
"Let queens and mystics and religious bees
Talk of such inconceivables as glass;
The blunt lay worker flies at what she sees,
Look there—ahead, ahead—the flowers, the grass!"
We catch her in a handkerchief (who knows
What rage she feels, what terror, what despair?)
And shake her out—and gaily out she goes
Where quivering flowers stand thick in summer air,
To drink their hearts. But left to her own will
She would have died upon the window-sill.'

"No Safe Investment"

THERE IS NO SAFE INVESTMENT. To love at all is to be vulnerable. Love anything, and your heart will certainly be wrung and possibly be broken. If you want to make sure of keeping it intact, you must give your heart to no one, not even to an animal. Wrap it carefully round with hobbies and little luxuries; avoid all entanglements; lock it up safe in the casket or coffin of your selfishness. But in that casket—safe, dark, motionless, airless —it will change. It will not be broken; it will become unbreakable, impenetrable, irredeemable. The alternative to tragedy, or at least to the risk of tragedy, is damnation. The only place outside Heaven where you can be perfectly safe from all the dangers and perturbations of love is Hell.

The Four Loves (New York: Harcourt, Brace and World, 1960), p. 169.

"We Shall Find Them All in Him"

I DARE NOT—and all the less because longings and
terrors of my own prompt me to do so—leave any be-
reaved and desolate reader confirmed in the widespread
illusion that reunion with the loved dead is the goal of
the Christian life. The denial of this may sound harsh
and unreal in the ears of the broken hearted, but it must
be denied.

"'Thou hast made us for thyself," said St. Augustine,
"and our heart has no rest till it comes to Thee." This,
so easy to believe for a brief moment before the altar or,
perhaps, half-praying, half-meditating in an April wood,
sounds like mockery beside a deathbed. But we shall be
far more truly mocked if, casting this way, we pin our
comfort on the hope—perhaps even with the aid of *séance*
and necromancy—of some day, this time forever, enjoying the earthly Beloved again, and no more. It is hard not
to imagine that such an endless prolongation of earthly
happiness would be completely satisfying.

But, if I may trust my own experience, we get at once
a sharp warning that there is something wrong. The moment we attempt to use our faith in the other world for
this purpose, that faith weakens. The moments in my life
when it was really strong have all been moments when
God Himself was central in my thoughts. Believing in
Him, I could then believe in Heaven as a corollary. But
the reverse process—believing first in reunion with the

The Four Loves, pp. 188–91.

Beloved, and then, for the sake of that reunion, believing in Heaven, and finally, for the sake of Heaven, believing in God—this will not work. One can of course imagine things. But a self-critical person will soon be increasingly aware that the imagination at work is his own; he knows he is only weaving a fantasy. And simpler souls will find the phantoms they try to feed on void of all comfort and nourishment, only to be stimulated into some semblance of reality by pitiful efforts of self-hypnotism, and perhaps by the aid of ignoble pictures and hymns and (what is worse) witches.

We find thus by experience that there is no good applying to Heaven for earthly comfort. Heaven can give heavenly comfort; no other kind. And earth cannot give earthly comfort either. There is no earthly comfort in the long run.

For the dream of finding our end, the thing we were made for, in a Heaven of purely human love could not be true unless our whole Faith were wrong. We were made for God. Only by being in some respect like Him, only by being a manifestation of His beauty, lovingkindness, wisdom or goodness, has any earthly Beloved excited our love. It is not that we have loved them too much, but that we did not quite understand what we were loving. It is not that we shall be asked to turn from them, so dearly familiar, to a Stranger. When we see the face of God we shall know that we have always known it. He has been a party to, has made, sustained and moved moment by moment within, all our earthly experiences of innocent love. All that was true love in them was, even on earth, far more His than ours, and ours only because His. In

Heaven there will be no anguish and no duty of turning away from our earthly Beloveds. First, because we shall have turned already; from the portraits to the Original, from the rivulets to the Fountain, from the creatures He made lovable to Love Himself. But secondly, because we shall find them all in Him. By loving Him more than them we shall love them more than we now do.

But all that is far away in "the land of the Trinity," not here in exile, in the weeping valley.

Conclusion:
Realism or Idealism?

CLEARLY, THE GREATEST QUESTION IS: What is the meaning of life?

There are two kinds of answers: realistic and idealistic.

Realistic answers are gritty and earthy. They say that life is bloody birth and bloody death and bloody bad between. They remind us that we stand on dirt, not air. They tell us, "Dust thou art, and unto dust thou shalt return."

Idealistic answers are full of wonder and hope. They say that we are made of star-stuff and that earth is a colony of Heaven. They remind us that we breathe air, not dirt. They pipe to us music that is an echo from Eden.

Materialism, existentialism, atheism, scientism, cynicism, and stoicism are realisms. Platonism, Hinduism, Buddhism, Taoism, Rationalism, Romanticism, and the New Age Movement are idealisms.

Christianity alone is both. It is more realistic than any other realism and more idealistic than any other idealism. With Plato it sends us from the cave of shadows up to the Heavenly light. Then, with Christ, it sends us down to a stable full of cow dung and a Cross full of nails.

And then it sends us to the marriage chamber of Infinite Joy Himself for ecstasy unending and unutterable.

Suggestions for Further Reading

The five sections of this book offer samples of C. S. Lewis' writing about five of the deepest questions in human life:

1. Is this world of shadows all there is?
2. What do we really want, deep down?
3. What is Heaven, really?
4. How do you get there?
5. Don't pain and suffering refute this "fairy tale"?

For more explorations of these five fascinating caves, you may want to try the following seven books, six of them by the editor of this anthology and all of them heavily indebted to Lewis:

1. *Chance or the Dance?* by Thomas Howard (San Francisco: Ignatius Press, 1989).

2. *Heaven, the Heart's Deepest Longing* by Peter Kreeft (San Francisco: Ignatius Press, 1989).

3. *Everything You Ever Wanted to Know about Heaven But Never Dreamed of Asking* by Peter Kreeft (San Francisco: Ignatius Press, 1990).

4. *Between Heaven and Hell* by Peter Kreeft (Ann Arbor, Mich: Inter Varsity Press, 1982), and *Socrates Meets Jesus* by Peter Kreeft (San Francisco: Ignatius Press, 1995).

5. *Making Sense Out of Suffering* by Peter Kreeft (Ann Arbor, Mich.: Servant Publications, 1986) and *Love Is Stronger Than Death* by Peter Kreeft (San Francisco: Ignatius Press, 1992).

But it would be far better to read more of Lewis. I will not pick out just a few of his fifty books for you, for (1) *everything* his pen touches turns to gold, and (2) different readers seek different kinds or genres of gold. But here is a list of his major titles, all still in print. If your local bookstore does not stock any given in-print book, the staff can order it for you. If not, try another bookstore.

In compiling this bibliography of C. S. Lewis' writings, I have used the unscholarly but practical device of anticipating the reader's likely interests. To this end, I have (1) listed American rather than British editions in most cases, (2) listed paperback rather than hardcover editions wherever available, (3) arranged the books by genre, and (4) starred items especially recommended.

Religion and Philosophy:

The Problem of Pain. New York: Macmillan, 1978.

The Screwtape Letters. New York: Macmillan, 1982.

Mere Christianity. New York, Macmillan, 1978.

The Abolition of Man. New York: Macmillan, 1978.

Miracles: A Preliminary Study. New York: Macmillan, 1978.

Reflections on the Psalms. New York: Walker & Co., 1985.

The Four Loves. New York: Harcourt Brace Jovanovich, 1971.

Letters to Malcolm: Chiefly on Prayer. New York: Harcourt Brace Jovanovich, 1973.

Collections of Essays:

The Weight of Glory and Other Addresses. New York: Macmillan, 1980.

The World's Last Night and Other Essays. New York: Harcourt Brace Jovanovich, 1973.

They Asked for a Paper: Papers and Addresses. London: G. Bles, 1962.

Of Other Worlds: Essays and Stories. New York: Harcourt Brace Jovanovich, 1975.

Christian Reflections. Grand Rapids, Mich.: Wm. B. Eerdmans, 1968.

God in the Dock. Grand Rapids, Mich.: Wm. B. Eerdmans, 1970.

Present Concerns. New York: Harcourt Brace Jovanovich, 1975.

POEMS:

Poems. New York: Harcourt Brace Jovanovich, 1977.

Narrative Poems. New York: Harcourt Brace Jovanovich, 1979.

AUTOBIOGRAPHICAL:

Surprised by Joy: The Shape of My Early Life. New York: Harcourt Brace Jovanovich, 1966.

A Grief Observed. New York: Bantam, 1976.

Letters, W. H. Lewis, ed. New York: Harcourt Brace Jovanovich, 1966.

Letters to an American Lady. Grand Rapids, Mich.: Wm. B. Eerdmans, 1967.

C. S. Lewis' Letters to Children, ed. Lyle W. Dorsett and Marjorie Mead. New York: Macmillan, 1985.

CHILDREN'S FICTION:

The Chronicles of Narnia, 7 books, including *The Lion, the Witch and the Wardrobe; Prince Caspian; The Voyage of the Dawn*

Treader; The Silver Chair; The Horse and His Boy; The Magician's Nephew; The Last Battle. New York: Macmillan, 1986.

ADULT FICTION:

The Pilgrim's Regress: An Allegorical Apology for Christianity, Reason, and Romanticism. New York: Bantam, 1981.

*The Space Trilogy, 3 vols., including *Out of the Silent Planet*; *Perelandra*; and *That Hideous Strength*. New York: Macmillan, 1986.

*Till We Have Faces: A Myth Retold. New York: Harcourt Brace Jovanovich, 1980.

*The Great Divorce. New York: Macmillan, 1978.

LITERARY HISTORY AND CRITICISM:

The Allegory of Love: A Study in Medieval Tradition. New York: Oxford University Press, 1958.

Rehabilitation and Other Essays. Folcroft, Penn.: Folcroft Press, 1969.

*A Preface to "Paradise Lost". New York: Oxford University Press, 1942.

English Literature in the Sixteenth Century, Excluding Drama (vol. III of *The Oxford History of English Literature*). Oxford: Clarendon Press, 1954.

An Experiment in Criticism. New York: Cambridge University Press, 1961.

Studies in Medieval and Renaissance Literature, collected by Walter Hooper. Cambridge: Cambridge University Press, 1966.

Selected Literary Essays, edited by Walter Hooper. Cambridge: Cambridge University Press, 1964.

Studies in Words. Cambridge: Cambridge University Press, 1960.

The Discarded Image: An Introduction to Medieval and Renaissance Literature. Cambridge: Cambridge University Press, 1964.

On Stories and Other Essays on Literature. New York: Harcourt Brace Jovanovich, 1982.

Spenser's Images of Life. Cambridge: Cambridge University Press, 1967.

Acknowledgments

Permission to reprint excerpts from the following works by C. S. Lewis is gratefully acknowledged:

The Allegory of Love: A Study in Medieval Tradition. A Galaxy Book. New York: Oxford University Press, copyright 1958. Reprinted with permission of Oxford University Press, Oxford, England.

The Four Loves. A Harvest/HBJ Book. New York and London: Harcourt, Brace and World, copyright 1960 by Helen Joy Lewis. Reprinted with permission of Harcourt Brace Jovanovich.

God in the Dock: Essays on Theology and Ethics. Edited by Walter Hooper. Grand Rapids, Michigan: William B. Eerdmans, copyright 1970 by the Trustees of the Estate of C. S. Lewis. Reprinted with permission of HarperCollins Publishers Limited, London.

The Great Divorce. New York, Macmillan and Company, copyright 1946. Reprinted with permission of HarperCollins Publishers Limited, London.

A Grief Observed. New York: Seabury Press, copyright 1961 by N. W. Clerk. Reprinted with permission of HarperCollins Publishers, New York.

The Last Battle. New York: Macmillan Company, copyright 1956. Reprinted with permission of HarperCollins Publishers Limited, London.

Letters to an American Lady. Edited by Clyde S. Kilby. Grand Rapids, Michigan: William B. Eerdmans Publishing Company, copyright 1967. Reprinted with permission of William B. Eerdmans.

Letters to Malcolm: Chiefly on Prayer. New York: Harcourt, Brace and World, copyright 1963, 1964 by the Estate of C. S. Lewis and/or C. S. Lewis. Reprinted with permission of Harcourt Brace Jovanovich.

The Lion, the Witch and the Wardrobe: A Story for Children. New York: Macmillan Company, copyright 1950. Reprinted with permission of HarperCollins Publishers Limited, London.

Mere Christianity. Collier Books. New York: Macmillan Company, copyright 1943, 1945, 1952. Reprinted with permission of HarperCollins Publishers Limited, London.

Perelandra: A Novel. New York: Macmillan Company, copyright 1952, 1961. Reprinted with permission of Random House UK Limited.

The Pilgrim's Regress: An Allegorical Apology for Christianity, Reason, and Romanticism. Grand Rapids, Michigan: William B. Eerdmans Company, copyright 1933, 1943 by Clive Staples Lewis. Reprinted with permission of William B. Eerdmans.

Poems. Edited by Walter Hooper. New York: Harcourt Brace and World, copyright 1964 by the Executors of the Estate of C. S. Lewis. Reprinted with permission of Harcourt Brace Jovanovich.

The Problem of Pain. Collins, Fount Paperbacks. Glasgow: William Collins Limited, 1949. Copyright 1940 by C. S.

Lewis, Pte. Ltd. Reprinted with permission of Harper-Collins Publishers Limited, London.

The Silver Chair. New York: Macmillan Company, copyright 1953. Reprinted with permission of HarperCollins Publishers Limited, London.

Surprised by Joy: The Shape of My Early Life. A Harvest Book. New York and London: Harcourt, Brace and World, copyright 1955 by C. S. Lewis. Reprinted with permission of Harcourt Brace Jovanovich.

Till We Have Faces: A Myth Retold. New York: Harcourt Brace and Company, 1956. Reprinted with permission of Harcourt Brace Jovanovich.

The Voyage of the Dawn Treader. New York: Macmillan Company, 1952. Reprinted with permission of HarperCollins Publishers Limited, London.

The Weight of Glory and Other Addresses. New York: Macmillan Company, copyright 1949. Reprinted with permission of HarperCollins Publishers Limited, London.

We also gratefully acknowlege the following:

George MacDonald, *The Golden Key.* With pictures by Maurice Sendak, Afterword by W. H. Auden. New York: Farrar, Straus and Giroux, 1967.

Lint Hatcher, Introduction to "The Golden Key". *Wonder* magazine, Spring 1990.